Over the past three decades, vegan dairy expert Miyoko Schinner has figured out the best way to make plant-based milk products mimic real dairy, and she is now ready to share these meticulously curated recipes. In *The Vegan Creamery,* you'll learn to use the age-old concepts of culturing to make French-Style Soft Truffle Cheese, perfect on a charcuterie board, and fermenting plant-based milk to create Reggie Goat Cheese, a tangy spread that is delicious atop pizza. You'll use atypical plant-based ingredients like watermelon seed kernel milk to make mozzarella and mung beans to make Halloumi. Alongside these delectable dairy-free cheese creations, you'll learn to make Pumpkin Seed–Oat Yogurt to serve with a bowl of fresh fruit or Salted Maple Chocolate Chip Cookie Dough Ice Cream to satisfy your cravings for a rich dessert.

With Schinner's recipes, you'll discover how to craft beautiful vegan food for everyday life that will expand your palate and help save the planet. *The Vegan Creamery* is just the cookbook to guide you on your plant-based journey.

THE
Vegan Creamery

Miyoko Schinner

PHOTOGRAPHS BY EVA KOLENKO
FOREWORD BY JOE YONAN

THE
Vegan Creamery

PLANT-BASED CHEESE,
MILK, ICE CREAM,
AND MORE

TEN SPEED PRESS
California | New York

CONTENTS

FOREWORD

The first time I met Miyoko Schinner, we talked about mold. You might not think it would be the best choice of dinner topics, but the subject was the fungus whose spores create the moldy veins—and flavor—of some of the world's best blue cheeses.

Miyoko was excited to show me the results of her latest experiments, including a vegan blue cheese that differed from its conventional counterparts in one obvious and one not-so-obvious way. It was based on cashews instead of milk; that's the obvious part. What was so groundbreaking was also less visible: She had inoculated her cashew blend with *Penicillium roqueforti,* making this the first vegan cheese I had heard of, let alone tasted, that incorporated such artisanal, traditional techniques.

The results spoke for themselves: a characteristically tangy funk whose flavor made this the blue-cheesiest vegan cheese I had ever tasted. While some other vegan cheesemakers were relying solely on flavor additives, Miyoko was letting nature and time do much of the work.

With the company she founded, Miyoko went on to make a raft of innovative nondairy products, including a cultured vegan butter that was the first such spread I could not only eat on bread by itself but also devour happily that way, not to mention use it in such butter-forward recipes as shortbread. And rather than keep trying to get the stretchability and meltability of mozzarella in vegan form, she developed a version for pizza that starts off as a liquid instead of needing to transform into one in the oven. How brilliant is that?

Over the years, I've had the pleasure of sharing meals, phone calls, and Zoom interviews with Miyoko, and so when I decided to write a treatise on plant-based cooking as its own cuisine, I knew I'd want to pick her brain. I ended up collaborating with her on recipes for butter, "goat" cheese rolled in herbs, pumpkin seed ricotta, and more. In fact, her ricotta recipe was so surprising—it didn't require any lemon or other acidic ingredient for the seed-and-nut blend to form curds—that I riffed on it to make a pumpkin seed tofu.

Anyone who has met Miyoko knows just how passionate she is about providing consumers with vegan alternatives. What I want to make sure everyone also realizes is just how generous she is with her hard-won knowledge and how she never stops innovating. Her 2012 book, *Artisan Vegan Cheese,* helped spark a revolution in plant-based cheesemaking, inspiring makers the world over to start culturing and fermenting their own vegan cheeses. But when she thought about revising it, she realized that she had learned so much in the intervening dozen years that it was time for an entirely new take.

In case you haven't figured it out yet, Miyoko Schinner is many things—entrepreneur, animal advocate, author, researcher—but perhaps more than anything she is a teacher. At Rancho Compasión, the farmed animal sanctuary she founded almost a decade ago, she incorporates a youth education program. She recently started teaching at UC Berkeley's Plant Futures Challenge Lab, which works to connect academics with plant-based businesses. And with this book she wants to help me, you, and anyone else who's interested to find ways to make dairy alternatives so delicious you wouldn't hesitate to serve them to guests, even nonvegan ones.

I invite you to read, learn, and, most important, cook. What will you make first? And what revolution will Miyoko's approach spark next?

—*Joe Yonan*

INTRODUCTION: MY STORY

If Helen of Troy was the face that launched a thousand ships, I hope this is the book that launches a thousand vegan creameries around the world, each serving its own community. Even more, I hope this book inspires people in home kitchens everywhere to discover the magic that lies in plant milks.

Many have generously given my first book, *Artisan Vegan Cheese,* the credit for lighting the way for many to explore the subject, and in truth, there are vegan cheesemongers the world over who took their inspiration from my book. I have visited some of them in far-flung places, such as Budapest, London, Genoa, Rome, and Kyoto, and have delighted in meeting them and tasting their creations. Initially, I thought I'd just do a revised edition of that book, but as I leafed through my own cashew milk–stained copy, I realized that in just over a decade from when I wrote it, my understanding of the science and artistry of plant-milk dairy had evolved so much that it needed a total rewrite.

We are still in the nascency of this exploration. Whereas humankind has had thousands of years to explore the functionality of animal milks, our knowledge of what's possible with plant milks is very, very limited. This is especially true for cheese, often considered the last frontier. For these reasons, this is likely the hardest book I have ever written, and I still feel that I'm midstream in recipe development. But I am hoping it will inspire others to forge on.

My goal is to ignite passion in people to dig deeper, explore further, become more curious about the things we could do with various plant milks, to understand how their proteins, fats, and other nutrients function and react in different combinations and environments. While this book contains some methodologies that I believe are new, it is by no means *the* treatise on everything plant dairy. After all, I, too, am just an early explorer, trying to understand as much as I can. But what I have come to understand, I want to share with everyone. If we are to change the food system and find more compassionate ways to produce traditional foods without animal milk, then we need to make the information available to as many people as possible and not hoard it for ourselves or our companies.

Before we plunge further into the ins and outs of plant milk, I'd like to meander down, shall we say, "memory lane," and explain why it was unlikely that a Japanese woman born in a country at a time when dairy products were practically nonexistent would have become obsessed with all things cheese and butter, even earning the unofficial title of Queen of Vegan Cheese and Butter. I began my life in the land of rice and soy sauce—oh, and *natto,* those stinky, stretchy, fermented soybeans only people from the Kanto area (where Tokyo and Yokohama are located) would eat. I was a natto-girl all the way, devouring them on a hot bowl of rice for breakfast. Perhaps it was my taste for natto that prepared me for the stinkiest, strongest cheeses later in life.

When I was seven, we moved to a sleepy town in Northern California (not so sleepy now), from an even sleepier village in Japan. Everything I saw in Mill Valley was exotic and somehow beautiful. My mom and I would walk down to Bill's corner store across the street from my elementary school, and she'd treat me to Pixy Stix, those straws with the colorful sugary powder in them that would tingle in your mouth— pure magic. I would stare at blue-eyed, blond children—I was convinced they were made from angel dust. I, on the other hand, with my black hair and flat face, had been made of, well, natto.

I wanted so badly to be just like those golden kids. I thought I'd have my chance the first time I had pizza at a party I'd been invited to—one bite, I thought, and I'd be transformed. And there it was: a giant round thing glistening in oil. There's an expression in Japan to describe how Westerners smell—*bata-kusai,* or "stinks of butter." (Likewise, there's an equivalent expression to describe the smell of Japanese— *shoyu-kusai*—or "stinks of soy sauce.") As I watched the kids grabbing slice after slice, I stood there, repulsed by its pungent smell. But I bravely approached the table and hesitantly took a bite. The oil dripped down my mouth and coated my throat. I gagged. I didn't understand—*how could anyone like something so disgusting?* I thought. The worst part was that I didn't even go blond.

Fast-forward to high school. I had moved beyond onigiri and umeboshi and somehow, after that first horrible pizza experience, had become obsessed with cheese. This was the 1970s, and while most of my friends stuck to cheddar, Monterey Jack, and Swiss, or worse—American cheese—I had become a full-blown cheese adventurer, perhaps even a snob, snickering at the Velveeta in the fridges of my friends, Thanks to my dad, a white man born in Charlotte, raised in Kansas City, then shipped off in high school to live with his aunt in her hotel in Santa Cruz, my fridge at home was filled with the likes of Brie, Camembert, Roquefort, and even Limburger, the unabashedly stinky cheese that repulsed all of my friends.

My dad and I would sometimes drive to the Marin French Cheese Company in West Marin, the oldest cheese company in America. Tucked away in the pastoral countryside, the place seemed so remote at the time but is literally 5 minutes from where I live now. We'd stock up on their lovely bloomy rind cheeses, packed traditionally in round wooden boxes with their Rouge et Noir logo.

I went on to college, where I started hosting wine and cheese parties in my dorm room on Friday nights, procuring as many exotic cheeses as I could from the one and only specialty food shop in town. After sophomore year, a girlfriend and I decided to take a gap year and backpack around Europe for a few months. This was where the real awakening took place. I remember arriving in Paris and stumbling into my first cheese shop. My memory paints a picture of walls covered with shelves to the ceiling, filled with cheeses of every variety—I realize now that it wouldn't have been possible, since they would have had to have been refrigerated. But that is the indelible, if factually incorrect, memory I've held on to. In this paradise of fromage, I didn't even know where to start. I had never seen most of them. We filled our basket with cheeses of various shapes and textures, some hard, some seemingly oozing out of their film. Then off we went to a grassy pitch by the side of a road to unwrap our treasures and eat them with chunks of Parisian baguette, washing it all down with a bottle of cheap red wine. Ahh—what more could I ask for? To me, that moment embodied the Good Life. I mean, what else was there?

Over the next six months, from England down to Greece, we sought out cheese in every corner of Europe. What struck me profoundly then was something that amazes me to this day: the simple fact that the thousands of varieties of cheese all over the world are based on one ingredient—milk, whether from a cow, goat, or sheep (and sometimes from even more exotic animals, such as camels or even humans). To the milk are added enzymes and bacteria, and sometimes yeasts and molds, and then nature does its thing, transforming, through chemical and biological reactions, liquid milk into cheese.

Beyond the types of bacteria, yeast, or mold added to the milk, there are even environmental considerations, such as temperature and humidity to consider, as well as whether there are other things in the environment, such as *Penicillium roqueforti,* perhaps floating around the air from some moldy bread. Then there is the matter of the nutritional makeup of the milk itself: What is the fat content of the milk? Were the cows milked in the winter or summer? All of these variables play a part in the outcome of the cheese.

Cheese is an evolutionary science that has gone on in the rustic "kitchen labs" of farmhouses and homes of everyday people for thousands of years. It is also an art form that people have perfected after observing what nature can do to milk, a living craft that requires constant attention. The head cheesemaker at Cowgirl Creamery told me once how cheese was "alive," and therefore needed daily monitoring. It isn't just a recipe or formula you follow; the temperature, humidity, the fat and protein content of the milk—all of this can alter the "recipe." Master cheesemakers know how to make adjustments to achieve similar results each time because it is an art form as well as a science.

Today, the biggest cheese companies have found ways to mass-produce cheese, bypassing many of the traditional methods, such as the long aging required for hard cheeses like cheddar, using adjuncts (added ingredients such as fillers and gums) to create in days what used to take months. A hundred years ago, the average American ate four pounds of cheese per year; in the 1970s, eleven pounds; and today, more than forty pounds, and hence, manufacturers have learned to crank it out. Real estate is costly, and that Parmesan taking up space in your aging room for two years becomes very expensive. To cut costs, they have even found ways to turn the waste stream, that is, the whey, into cheese: Yep, all that Velveeta, those Kraft Singles, and other processed cheeses that line grocery walls contain lists of ingredients that would shock your great grandmother: Water, Salt, Artificial Coloring, Flavorings, Lecithin, Enzyme Modified Cheese, Dehydrated Cream, Anhydrous Milk-Fat, Phosphoric Acid, Albumin from Cheese Whey, Acetic Acid, Monosodium Phosphate, Potassium Citrate, Sodium Tartrate, Potassium Sorbate. You get the idea.

But let's return to my story. After college, I moved back to Japan. I wanted to reconnect with a part of my life that I felt had been lost, even to myself: The little girl who loved to dip nori in soy sauce and wrap it around hot rice. The girl who couldn't wait for *o-shogatsu*, or New Year's, to hear the *taiko* drumming and eat *o-zoni,* or mochi soup. The girl who ran out into the street with excitement when the sweet potato monger rolled by with his coal-laden cart of smoky *ishi-yaki-imo*.

Tokyo was a bit bigger than the village where I had grown up in a two-story, traditional Japanese house with sliding *fusuma* doors that opened up to a rice paddy. It seemed bigger, busier, more bustling than even New York. At first, I lived with my aunt and uncle next to a freeway in the "burbs," which were really just a congested mangle of concrete buildings that stretched between Tokyo and Yokohama. I concentrated on trying to relearn Japanese, much of which I'd forgotten, and to learn how to read and write *kanji*. The first few months were fun: I wanted to do and taste everything that was Japanese.

But as the months wore on, I began to grow tired of the bowls of noodles and rice and pickles and everything tasting of soy sauce. I yearned for, well, the scents of butter, heavy cream, and cheese. I mentioned this to my aunt, who went to the supermarket and brought back a little packet of processed cheese slices. This was all there was, she said. The truth is that dairy was not a part of the traditional Asian diet until recently. I hadn't had milk as a child in Japan. In fact, the only other dairy memory from childhood was the time my mother took me to eat ice cream for the first time. She told me we were going someplace special, and so we got all dressed up and took a cab instead of the train. At a fancy restaurant, I was served a parfait bowl with one perfect scoop of vanilla ice cream. It was nothing short of mystical and magical—I concentrated so hard on that scoop, my mouth caressing each spoonful, eating as slowly as possible to make the experience last as long as possible before it melted.

After a few months of living with my aunt and uncle, I left their little abode under a freeway and managed to find an apartment in the Roppongi district of Tokyo, an area known for its nightlife, smack-dab in the middle of everything happening. Restaurants, clubs, trendy boutiques—they were all there. One day, I stumbled upon a store called Meiji-ya, a specialty store carrying tons of imported items. Among them was an entire cooler of cheese! Soft cheese, hard cheese, stinky cheese, moldy cheese! I could not believe it. I walked out of Meiji-ya with Brie and some fancy crackers, and celebrated life all over again. Yes, it was expensive, but I knew that I could once again satisfy my addiction.

Oh, speaking of addiction—I'm not just speaking metaphorically. Dairy products are *literally* addictive. Cow's milk contains something called casomorphin, an actual opioid, and because cheese is a concentrated form of milk, there's a super dose of it in cheese. Yup. That's why so many people say, "I could go vegan, but I can't give up cheese!" It almost sounds like *queso + morphine,* a liquid cheese that you might shoot up. It's an opioid that is released when casein, a milk protein, breaks down in your body. So when you say that you can't give up cheese, it's not just because it tastes great, it's because it's truly biologically addicting.

In the 1980s, the Japanese were enamored with everything French, including its cuisine, and there were numerous French restaurants within walking distance of my apartment. In fact, there were more Michelin-starred restaurants in Tokyo than in all of France. (The Japanese are great improvers—they borrow from other cultures and then make it better.) Thousands of miles from Europe, in the most unlikely place, I became obsessed with French cuisine. At an international bookstore, I bought a copy of *Mastering the Art of French Cooking,* and started to cook my way through it, trying to vegetarianize all the dishes. Butter, heavy cream, and cheese were back on my table, and they found their way into everything I made.

And then something happened. One day I saw an article describing the abuses in the dairy industry. While I had always thought dairy cows just grazed happily in the grass, this article suggested otherwise. I decided then and there that I would try to eliminate all animal products from my diet. I went vegan.

But how was I to cook without glorious butter that browned when melted and could "fix" any recipe gone wrong? How would I replace the magical richness conferred by heavy cream? And what would I serve with wine if not cheese?

I dove into deep experimentation. I hosted vegan dinner parties every Friday night, creating ten- to twelve-course tasting menus, inviting everyone and anyone I knew, who then would invite others, which led to magazine features and cooking demos at department stores. Eventually, I'd accumulated enough recipes to write a book, which I did in Japanese.

But finding a way to make vegan cheese eluded me. Then one day I saw a Japanese TV show about some Buddhist nuns treating tofu in unique ways. For one dish, they covered the tofu in ash and left it to ferment for a month. In another, they buried it in miso for a day or two, which changed the texture from crumbly to smooth and buttery. I tried it at home. It certainly was cheese-like, although far too salty. I played around with it and modified the recipe to include wine (for a little acidity) and mirin, or sweet sake, to give it umami and round out the flavors. This was a huge hit at the next Friday night party, where I served it with crostini and roasted vegetables.

Tofu is sometimes called soy cheese because it is made in a very similar process to cheese. Soy milk is heated and then an enzyme is added—traditionally

Above left: Rufus and Reggie, the OGs (original goats), aka "the boyfriend goats" who kicked it all off

Above right: Angel the cow, the diva of the sanctuary, with Echo the goose, her royal guardsman

magnesium chloride from seawater, but also calcium sulfate or even lemon juice. The minerals or acid coagulate the proteins to form curds, and then the whey is drained off. The curds are poured into forms and pressed, just the way cheese is made. What's missing is the lactic acid bacteria that lowers the pH and turns the sweetness of the milk to something more acidic and savory, the hallmarks of cheese. In other words, cheese is fermented, but tofu is not (although the Chinese do have something called fermented tofu, which is very similar in texture to the miso-covered cheese described here—buttery, smooth, and definitely funky in flavor).

In my mind, it seemed to make so much sense, and yet the reality was different: If soy milk coagulates, then why couldn't it be used to make cheese? And why were the resulting curds so different from that of cow's milk? This question plagued me. I didn't understand that it had to do with the difference in protein types between cow's milk and soy milk. Mammalian milk, but particularly cow's milk, contains the almost-magical casein, responsible for that famous stretch in cheese. (Goat's milk, by the way, has almost 90 percent less casein than cow's milk, which is why it doesn't have the same stretch.) It would be many years before I could spend the time to really delve deeply into plant protein fermentation and begin to understand the differences in their behavior.

Now fast-forward into the 1990s, and I'm back in the US of A. I'd opened a vegan bakery, which turned into a vegan restaurant, which turned into a natural food company making "alternative meats," years before it became a thing. But cheese? At the restaurant, I'd developed an oat-based melty concoction atop lasagna as well as seitan Parmesan. But unctuous, luscious, creamy, funky stuff? Not yet.

The funny thing is that over the years my tastes had changed, and I'd lost my addiction and craving for cheese. But every time I prepared appetizers for a dinner party, it bothered me that I had no vegan cheese to serve, and it bugged me even more that I hadn't yet developed any. At grocery stores, vegan cheese slices had begun to hit the shelves—stuff made of oil and starch, much like the processed cheese of the animal dairy world—and while the initial discovery was exciting, the products themselves left me feeling like I'd be settling for Velveeta.

I guess you might call it a midlife crisis. I had turned fifty. I had *a* good life— three great kids, a beautiful home, friends. But where was *the* good life, the one I had envisioned sitting on that grassy knoll in Paris savoring that lunch of delicious cheeses and bread? Where was my *cheese*?

So I got back in the kitchen. If there was to be great vegan cheese, I knew it had to be made using both science and artistry, embracing fermentation and methods of coagulation. Once again, I began thinking about the process for making tofu and knew there had to be a way to coagulate and ferment plant milks.

I started out by making cheese from soy yogurt. I'd learned to make dairy yogurt decades ago from an Egyptian cook in Cairo—I simply applied the technique to soy milk and found it worked beautifully. To make yogurt cheese, all you have to do is put natural yogurt (the kind without a bunch of gums and junk they put in yogurt today) in a muslin or cheesecloth bag and hang it from your faucet to drain for 12 to 24 hours. The resulting product is like a goat cheese and can be flavored or rolled in herbs or peppercorns or whatever delights you. One Christmas, at a party we threw, I served one of these yogurt-based cheeses and was asked by an impressed guest from which local creamery I had procured it.

I ventured beyond soy milk. I made milks and creams from anything and everything I could think of, including nuts of every sort, grains such as oats and sticky rice, and even legumes, with mixed degrees of success. I made cheese logs from cashews and melty cheeses from yogurt. The local junior college had cheesemaking courses, so I took a few to learn some of the science that I could perhaps apply to plant milks. My teenage kids were embarrassed to bring their friends home because there were cheeses at different stages of fermentation and aging all over my counters. I found a broken refrigerator that kept but one temperature—55°F—perfect for an aging room, and I practiced the art of affinage, or curing and aging cheese. I waxed some of them and laid them to rest for months or even years.

This led in 2012 to a book on the subject, *Artisan Vegan Cheese,* and eventually to a vegan cheese company, which quickly grew to being national. Today, there are a number of books and vegan cheese producers the world over. How quickly it has exploded! But we are all still explorers in this vast new territory of plant-milk products and recipes, and there is so much more to do!

This is the beginning of a new era as the world of dairy evolves from animal milk to plant milk, being reinterpreted for a kinder, more sustainable future. As human beings, we have an amazing opportunity to maintain our eating habits but do it in a more sustainable manner. Yes, we *can* have *the good life*—the compassionate dolce vita filled with all the rich and creamy delights we love while creating a better future for the planet, animals, and ourselves.

MY PHILOSOPHY
and the Simple Science Behind This New Frontier of Plant-Milk Products

What is "milk"? While Northern Europeans, specifically, have consumed animal-milk products for several thousand years, most of the world's populations have not. However, "milk" of a different kind was still consumed by many—but it was made from plants, such as soy, almonds, or even pistachios. Soy milk likely traces back more than 3,500 years, with the earliest reference from 1500 BC in a poem called "Ode to Tofu." Likewise, almond milk dates back more than 1,000 years from the Middle East, and coconut milk more than 5,000 years. To say that the term "milk" is reserved for the excretions of mammary glands from an animal is simply the hubris of a modern industry.

Still, we are in the nascency of this new wave, and what it all means is still a little unclear, as there is no standard. Whether we're talking about almond milk or vegan cheese, you'll find myriad approaches and ingredients. Commercial almond milk can be made from just almonds and water (sometimes containing only about six almonds per cup!) or it can contain a whole host of other ingredients, including gums, oils, and sugar. The vegan cheese slice on your burger could literally be a congealed concoction of saturated oils and starch with added flavors, offering no nutritional value whatsoever, or it could be a healthier version made from whole almonds. Manufacturers today have full license to make things however they want because there are no rules or standards, which puts the onus on the consumer to distinguish what's healthy and what's junk.

Beyond store shelves, you'll find different approaches by chefs and influencers. One might share a recipe for a wholesome fermented cream cheese made of pureed cashews, while another might make an instant version out of coconut oil, tapioca starch, and lemon juice that comes together in under five minutes.

So what's my philosophy in this new Wild, Wild West of plant-dairy foods? First of all, I am interested in basing my recipes on whole food ingredients as much as possible and am passionate about understanding how different plant milks behave and taste using different techniques. I love discovering new ways to utilize traditional plants in the kitchen. And let me emphasize the word *kitchen*—not a laboratory. I have a culinary approach to innovation, much as chefs do historically, finding different ways to make new things out of traditional ingredients and with techniques that are easily replicable. I believe that the answer to the future is adopting a democratic approach that is low cost and can be done by anyone with some simple kitchen appliances and access to readily available ingredients.

The techniques themselves give a proper nod to culinary history, while a few tweaks bring the science of cheesemaking into the present and carry it forward into the future. My respect for the art of fermentation is reflected in my approach to cheesemaking, so I don't shortcut this or "cheat" by adding acidic ingredients such as vinegar or lemon juice (unless needed for another reason, for coagulation or "bleaching" purposes to whiten a milk). Fermentation develops and reveals the full potential of plant milks, transforming them into yogurts with real tang or cheeses with umami flavors. Fermentation is an age-old natural process that proliferates healthy lactic acid bacteria while breaking down proteins and fats and making them more bioavailable, all while creating unique flavors. (Natural fermentation is not to be confused with so-called precision fermentation, a new technology that uses microorganisms to create specific proteins, such as actual milk proteins using yeasts.) And while my first plant dairy book, *Artisan Vegan Cheese,* delved into fermentation, I go much further in this book—actually coagulating the plant proteins to make curds and draining the whey, much as in traditional animal-milk cheesemaking.

I'd love to be a purist in the realm of plant dairy, using only the primary ingredients and adding nothing else, but we also have to remember that every seed, nut, and legume is distinct from others, with varying macro- and micronutrient profiles that don't all behave the same. For example, soy milk is similar to cow's milk in terms of fat and protein content, but the nature of the fats and protein differ between them, creating totally diverse results. Therefore, I've come to the conclusion that instead of constantly trying to mimic animal milk, we should honor and respect the unique qualities of each plant milk, letting them express their nature in each of these recipes and products. Yes, we'll get myriad results, but they can be myriad spectacular results.

We can create a new paradigm for plant-milk products, letting them express their own identity, rather than trying to force them to be a copycat of something from a cow. Even with these differences, these plant-milk recipes can still serve in the place of an established animal-milk product—whether it be a milk for your cereal, a sour

Techniques Used in This Book

In this book, everything starts with making milk from nuts, seeds, and legumes. You'll need a blender and a nut milk bag, and you'll be doing a lot of squeezing. While nut milk machines can be handy, they often require specific water-to-nut ratios, which may or may not work for many of the recipes. I've found that their ability to extract as much milk as possible is also limited, and a lot of milk is left in the pulp. Hence, you'll just need to develop some hand and arm muscles!

FERMENTATION

To make cheese, yogurt, sour cream, or many of the other fermented foods in this book, you'll be using bacterial cultures to ferment the milk (read more in Bacterial Cultures, page 27). In addition, you'll be coagulating the milk through various methods to make curds, and in many cases, draining the whey from the curds. And finally, you may be aging or ripening the cheese over a period of days, weeks, or even months. The journey at times is long, but the destination is worth it!

THE IMPORTANCE OF SANITATION

I can't emphasize enough the importance of sanitation. Fermentation requires creating the right environment for the intended bacteria to grow—but if the conditions are off, unwanted bacteria that can either be unhealthy or just taste bad can also grow. Kitchen implements should always be clean, but if you're making yogurt, cheese, sour cream, or anything else that requires fermentation, you should go a step further and actually sterilize your equipment, bowls, and even cheesecloth, unless the recipe already has a "kill step," meaning a heating step that will kill any unwanted organisms. For example, when the milk is heated high enough to form curds before fermentation, the equipment used prior to this step should be clean but does not need to be sterilized.

Boiling in water does magic. You can sterilize your jars, bowls, containers, silicone spatulas, and even cheesecloth and nut milk bags in a pot of boiling water for a couple of minutes prior to use. The recipes will tell you when you need a sterilized container or cheesecloth (when there is no kill step afterward). That's about it. Have a pot of boiling water going and get into the habit of incorporating this step, and your yogurt and cheese experiments will go beautifully.

cream to put on your tacos, or a cheese for your panini—and elicit excitement from the eater!

Plant-milk butter, yogurt, cheese, and more can be delicious *and* be their own category. Let's find new flavors, textures, and culinary opportunities that perhaps can't be replicated by animal milks as we establish a new tradition of foods that represent the wonders and flavors of the plant kingdom.

INGREDIENTS

Here, you'll find the whole food ingredients needed to make everything from milk to cheese. From the main actors—nuts, seeds, and legumes—to supporting players like shea butter and tapioca starch.

Nuts and Seeds

From the now ubiquitous cashews to the new-kid-on-the-block—watermelon seed kernels—a variety of nuts and seeds are used in this book to make everything from milk to cheese, sometimes in combination with vegetables or legumes. Each type of nut or seed has a different fatty acid profile and flavor, creating different curd sizes and flavors appropriate for different uses. The protein content can range from 20 to 30 percent or more, and many, such as hemp hearts, can contain a fatty acid ratio of omega-3 to omega-6 that is ideal.

Generally high in fiber as well, in most cases the milks will need to be strained before being coagulated. Some nut and seed milks coagulate, others do not. If they do coagulate, the curd sizes and textures will vary widely, all because the protein makeup differs in all of them. Sometimes I add a fat, such as melted coconut or shea butter, directly to the milk, which seems to "lock" the fat into the curds.

Note that all nuts and seeds here should be hulled, raw, and unsalted.

Cashews I have always thought of cashews as the "cow's milk" of the plant kingdom, being neutral in flavor and highly versatile. Cashews are a tropical nut, growing in the wild in many parts of the world. A mountain range I visited in Vietnam was literally covered in cashew trees as far as the eye could see, not planted by any human, though harvested and enjoyed by them. Cashews are a rain forest crop, and rainfall is their primary source of water, so if sourced carefully, cashews can be a very sustainable crop from an environmental standpoint. The shell, however, contains urushiol, a mild toxin, the same irritant found in poison ivy and poison oak. If not shelled carefully, either mechanically or with gloves, the toxin can irritate the hands of workers, often damaging the skin considerably after repeated exposure. This has been cited as human rights abuse for cashews in parts of the world, and hence I believe it is good to know from where and how your cashews were procured.

Because of their ease of use and versatility, cashews are the most widely used nuts for vegan cheesemaking. A soft nut, they puree into a fine cream without the need for straining to remove the pulp. Making cheese from cashews involves processing them into a paste rather than coagulating the milk; in fact, cashew milk is difficult to coagulate without the use of transglutaminase (see page 32).

Cashew-based cheeses and recipes are widely covered in my book *Artisan Vegan Cheese* as well as in books by many other authors. However, cashews seem to cause more allergies than many other nuts, so I have chosen to limit the number of cashew-based recipes in this book.

Almonds Almonds are grown throughout the world. While considered a water-intensive crop, they still require considerably less water than is required to produce animal milks. Almonds contain about 20 percent more protein than cashews and are a good source of calcium. Unlike cashew milk, almond milk needs to be strained to remove the pulp (which can be used to make delicious crackers and other recipes, see page 184) and will produce beautiful, satin-smooth but different-size curds using a variety of coagulants, ranging from lemon juice to calcium sulfate to transglutaminase. I use almonds in conjunction with other seeds, such as pumpkin, to create a variety of recipes.

Sunflower seeds Like cashews, they are very soft and hence can turn creamy easily but still need to be strained to remove the pulp. The flavor is fairly bland, which allows for easy taste adjustments. As a milk, it froths well for coffee drinks. The biggest issue is their color, which can turn brown and result in an off-colored cheese. Adding distilled white vinegar bleaches the color without adding a vinegary taste; I use this process in this book to make cheeses that are white.

Pumpkin seeds Shelled pumpkin seeds have a thin green skin, which, during the shelling process, sometimes gets partially removed, making it more attractive for cheese—if possible, select seeds that have less green in their skin. They have good curdling capabilities, but due to their color, I don't use them as the sole ingredient in a cheese. Store in a cool, dry place. For most recipes, the milk will need to be strained before using.

Hemp hearts These can be confusing because hulled hemp seeds are sometimes called "hemp seeds" and other times "hemp hearts," which are always *hulled* hemp hearts. In this book, we will call them "hemp hearts." Store in the refrigerator. When used alone, the milk will not need to be strained. Hemp hearts add richness and complexity to cheese.

Watermelon seed kernels (also known as watermelon seeds) These are not the black seeds in the watermelons of yesteryear before everything became seedless but are a white seed from a different variety of watermelon with little flesh. They are a common snack in China and are also grown in other parts of Asia, including India. When looking for this, make sure you aren't buying the kind of seeds for planting, but for snacking or eating. I have been able to find organic ones on Amazon, and an online cheese supply company (thecheesemaker.com) recently started carrying them as well; I predict they will become more widely available soon. If you search for them online, look for both watermelon seed kernels and watermelon seeds, as they are sold under both names. Their high protein content contributes to the structure of a cheese, but they can yield a slightly grassy flavor when fermented (which works well for some applications, such as Feta Fetish, page 141).

Watermelon seed kernels are high in a protein called albumin, also found in egg whites, which coagulates upon exposure to heat. This creates big, beautiful curds for cheesemaking.

Melon seeds In this case, I really do mean the seeds that you scrape out of your summer melon. They are fresh and soft and can produce delicious milk and cheese.

Legumes

Beans are generally very high in protein and carbohydrates while being low in fat. Soybeans, however, are high in fat and protein but low in starches. In this book, I use primarily soybeans, yellow split mung beans (moong dal), and chickpeas. In many cases, fats are added to create the proper mouthfeel for a cheese-like product.

These legumes cannot be used interchangeably, and the recipes *must be followed precisely.* Their high starch content adds viscosity and texture to recipes, such as in the Almond-Chickpea Yogurt (page 93), which is incredibly thick and creamy, or in my Malloumi (page 119), a moong dal ode to Halloumi.

Fermenting legumes can create a variety of flavors and smells, sometimes off-putting, often with an undesirable beany flavor as well, and without the familiar "dairy notes" that nuts or seeds can create. However, they can provide the perfect base for some recipes.

Soybeans Soybeans have been vilified in the United States for the myth of causing "man boobs" or cancer due to phytoestrogens, but they have been consumed throughout Asia for centuries. If soybeans truly caused cancer or "man boobs," we'd see many Asian men afflicted, which we don't. Also, cancer rates are lower in Asia than in the West. Lately, soybeans have gained popularity across Europe and other parts of the world.

Soybeans are a unique bean in that they mimic cow's milk in terms of their macronutrient profile, meaning that their relative percentages of protein, fat, and carbohydrates are very similar. For those without a soy allergy, organic soy products can be a very healthy addition to one's diet (I state the importance of buying organic here because of the commodification of soy in North America as a feed for animals, leading to vast amounts of GMO soy grown, which is damaging to the environment).

Tofu is often referred to as soy cheese because it is essentially made just like cheese—soy milk is heated, coagulated, and then made into blocks after separating the curds from the whey. The only difference is that tofu is not fermented. I did try coagulating soy milk after fermentation and found that the lower pH inhibited coagulation through traditional means. Still, it can be turned into cheese by first making it into yogurt (see Soy Yogurt Cheese, page 85) or combining it with other ingredients, such as watermelon seed kernels, to create cheeses such as Paneer (page 122), adding good nutrition along the way.

Chickpeas (garbanzo beans) Just the opposite of soy, these contain a high amount of starch and protein and virtually no fat at all. Trying to make chickpea bean milk in the same way as soy milk resulted in a bean sludge for me! But for this very reason, chickpeas create an incredibly thick yogurt that can be a substitute for soy yogurt for those trying to avoid soy. The starch helps create structure and texture for a few cheeses as well. In this book, I use whole chickpeas processed with water to make a thick milk, then remove fiber through straining to create an incredibly smooth mouthfeel without a beany flavor.

Moong dal (yellow split mung beans) A traditional ingredient in Indian cuisine, this is a very soft split bean that cooks very quickly. They are the base for both yogurt and the wonderful Malloumi (page 119), my answer to Halloumi.

Cultures, Adjuncts, and Supportive Ingredients

In this section, you'll learn about ingredients such as lactic acid bacteria, yeasts, and other microorganisms; and coagulants, starches, and oils that will help transform plant milk to yogurt, cheese, butter, and more.

BACTERIAL CULTURES

These are the primary drivers that turn your milk into yogurt, sour cream, or cheese. An entire book could be written (and many have been!) on different bacteria and their effects on food. There are literally thousands and thousands of bacteria, and different combinations produce different results (hence, producing the endless variety of cheeses worldwide). Some simply acidify milk while others produce specific flavor profiles, such as buttery or nutty notes, due to fats and proteins breaking down through fermentation. There is no way I can even begin to treat cultures with more than a few broad strokes here, as it can be a lifelong learning process even for cheesemakers.

Generally speaking, here's what happens in fermenting milks: Acidifying cultures eat the sugar in the milk and convert them to acid, lowering the pH; these are the bacteria responsible for converting a sweetish milk into something tangy and sharp, whether it be yogurt or cheese. There are thousands of bacteria that work their magic on various milks, and many are wild, floating in the air around us. Historically, cheeses and yogurts were made by utilizing natural bacteria and yeasts found in the environment. Today, culture companies have isolated and grown them, often in proprietary combinations specific to various applications and flavor profiles.

When I first wrote *Artisan Vegan Cheese,* there were no commercially available vegan cultures. Most commercial cultures were (and still are) grown in lactose, or milk sugar, and years ago, manufacturers had no reason to grow them in anything else, as they were used only to make animal-milk cheese—there was no vegan cheese industry at that time! To write my book, therefore, I utilized a fermented grain beverage called rejuvelac (see box on the next page), a sour concoction that captured the natural bacteria and yeasts in the environment. I include a recipe for rejuvelac here as well and offer it as an option for those who cannot obtain commercial cultures. At this point in my life, I'm happy to say that there are multiple sources for obtaining vegan cultures of every sort.

What does it mean for a culture to be vegan? Instead of being grown in lactose, they are grown in dextrose; some are even certified vegan. Those that are not certified can still be vegan, however. One way to know is to see if it is Kosher Parve (can be used with either dairy or meat per Jewish laws), or to look at the specification chart and determine if it is free of dairy allergens, which likely means that the culture used dextrose or another plant-based sugar rather than lactose but may simply not have been certified "vegan" by a third party.

REJUVELAC

This is a substitute for those who cannot obtain a commercial vegan culture. You can make this easily at home from most whole grains, although I recommend quinoa as the easiest and fastest way to make it.

Soak 1 cup (185g) of quinoa in water for at least 8 hours. Drain and place in a clean 1-quart (1L) jar. Cover the jar with cheesecloth and attach it with a rubber band. Keep this on your kitchen counter away from sunlight. Twice a day for 2 days, rinse the seeds in the jar and drain through the cheesecloth. In about 2 days, you should see tiny sprouts coming out of the quinoa (you will have to look very closely).

Now fill the jar with water and let it continue to sit on your counter for another 2 to 3 days until the water is cloudy and has a fermented smell. It should taste acidic, like lemon water. Strain it through a sieve and put it back in the jar. Now it is ready. You can store rejuvelac in the refrigerator for 2 to 3 weeks, or freeze it for later use (this does not affect its bacterial properties).

To use rejuvelac in place of a bacterial culture, add about ⅓ cup (80ml) to the recipe, reducing the water called for in the recipe by ⅓ cup (80ml).

It is important to note that rejuvelac cannot be heated beyond 120°F or so, or the bacteria will die. Therefore, rejuvelac can be used only in recipes for cheeses where the curds are not cooked. If the curds are cooked, add the rejuvelac later, at the time the recipe instructs you add the culture.

Bacterial cultures are loosely divided into two types depending on optimal temperature ranges for growing: mesophilic and thermophilic. Mesophilic cultures like lower temperatures, and are often the ones responsible for achieving buttery, cheesy notes. Thermophilic cultures like warmer temperatures and are often used for Italian-style cheeses as well as yogurt. Some cultures are a combination of both and can tolerate a wider temperature range. The specification sheets or the culture company will describe the ideal temperature for each, but a safe guide is to aim for 75° to 90°F for mesophilic and 90° to 110°F for thermophilic.

Culture companies are still trying to figure out how to maximize the flavors for various plant substrates, so what works beautifully for cashews may create the same flavor notes for pumpkin seeds. This is still a learning process for all. Let's remember we are still in the nascency of exploring plant milks and their attributes, while experimentation with animal milk has been going on for thousands of years.

Many people ask me if they can just use a probiotic capsule instead. Yes and no. Yes, they will acidify most milks. However, probiotic capsules aren't designed for flavor; they help create a healthy gut biome. Hence, the flavors that result can range from simply acidic to off-putting depending on what bacteria they use. I highly recommend looking into vegan cheese cultures, which are now readily available in many continents, including North America and Europe.

Other Fermented Foods

Other fermented foods, such as sauerkraut juice, kimchi, or nondairy yogurt can supplement or act as a substitute for bacterial cultures or rejuvelac in certain cases, as they contain live bacteria.

MOLDS AND YEASTS

To make some of the fancier cheeses in this book, such as those considered "bloomy rinds" and blue cheeses, various molds and yeasts are used.

Penicillium candidum or Penicillium camemberti These are the molds primarily responsible for the fuzzy white mold on the outside of classic Brie and Camembert, and can work for plant milks as well, although different milks react differently to these. They are also responsible for breaking down the proteins in the milk, which is why dairy bloomy rind cheeses get runnier over time. (This doesn't generally happen with cashew-based bloomy rind cheeses, which is why I have found a different milk base that does.) They are extremely sensitive not only to temperature but also to pH and humidity, and hence, the learning curve can be somewhat steep. If the humidity or the moisture content of the cheese itself is too high, for example, the intended mold may not grow but something else might, such as *Brevibacterium linens* (the red mold responsible for Muenster as well as stinky varieties such as Limburger). It may take practice to ensure the right conditions, but if you are patient, these can be among the most amazing cheeses to make.

Geotrichum candidum This is a yeast that raises pH and encourages mold growth, while adding valuable flavor as well. However, if out of balance with *Penicillium candidum*, it can lead to a wet rind and the growth of *Brevibacterium linens* as well. As a general rule, the ratio of *Geotrichum candidum* to *Penicillium candidum* should be no more than 1 to 10.

Penicillium roqueforti This is the blue mold responsible for blue cheese. As with all molds, it requires oxygen for growth, which is why blue cheese is usually poked with holes in order to stimulate its growth inside and not just the surface. In my experience, it also responds well to coconut oil, which is why the blue cheeses in this book contain that.

Cross-contamination between different molds can happen easily. Most cheese manufacturers will not make a white bloomy rind cheese in the same facility as blue cheese. At home, I have two wine fridges in different parts of the house where I ripen and age them apart to minimize cross-contamination. You can achieve this more simply by aging your wheels in separate containers with lids. However, it's inevitable that some cross-contamination will occur, and that's okay. You can scrape off the unwanted mold as you see it grow, and sometimes it may even add to the cheese itself. It's common for a blue to be "contaminated" by both *Penicillium candidum* and *Brevibacterium linens*. Just keep them in check by scraping them off the surface as they develop, which is what many cheesemakers do.

There are unwanted, unhealthy molds that can take root in your cheese, especially if proper sanitation methods are not maintained. Over time, you will learn which "uninvited" molds are unhealthy and which are just annoying and affect the quality of your cheese.

FATS AND OILS

Even though many nuts and seeds are high in fat, their composition is such that they generally do not behave similarly to cow's milk in terms of melting or, strangely enough, provide a rich mouthfeel. For this reason, some form of oil is added when needed for texture or functionality. In most commercial vegan cheeses, the choice of oil has been either coconut or palm oil, both highly saturated, with the latter also being a major contributor to the destruction of rain forest habitats. If I can achieve a desired flavor or texture without the addition of oil, that is always my first choice.

Coconut oil (refined or deodorized) Coconut oil, while praised by those on a keto diet, has come under the microscope lately for its unhealthy fatty acid profile (high in lauric acid, suspected of raising cholesterol). Coconut oil melts at under 76°F, which makes it unstable in warm environments, which is also why some artisan-style vegan cheeses end up as a puddle of oil on a warm day. Its melting curve is also rapid, unlike dairy fat, meaning that it turns liquid in your mouth quickly, rather than lingering. I do use coconut oil where appropriate, such as for the blue cheeses, but utilize a variety of fats depending on the recipe. In choosing coconut oil, use "refined" or "deodorized," never virgin coconut oil, which will just make your cheese or butter taste like coconuts.

Shea butter (preferably naturally refined or deodorized) Shea butter, extracted from a small nut from a wild tree historically thought to enhance health and youth, is generally known in the West only for its use in beauty products. However, it has been used in the kitchens of Africa for centuries, being made in homes through a simple boiling process. Shea butter, in its unrefined form, can have a strong aroma and a nutty flavor, while the refined form is very neutral. I have found that the color can vary from a rich gold to an ivory, depending on the source. It can also be somewhat grainy, especially the refined variety, which has to do with shea's different fatty acids melting at different temperatures. (If you end up buying a grainy shea butter, you will need to temper it. Simply melt it completely, stirring well, then refrigerate to cool down quickly. It will become smooth.)

Shea butter has a slightly waxy consistency and a melting curve similar to dairy fat, and hence lends great texture to certain cheeses. However, if used in excess, shea butter can make cheese too waxy. Shea butter melts between 90° and 100°F, so cheeses made with this hold up better in warmer weather than ones made with coconut oil. Shea butter is about 50 percent saturated fat, with almost all of that coming from stearic acid, the least damaging of saturated fats.

Cocoa butter (refined or deodorized) Cocoa butter, or the fat removed from the cacao bean, is the hardest and most temperature stable, with a melting point of 100°F or higher. In its hard state, it is a brittle fat that melts into a buttery liquid. I often use this in combination with shea to provide firmness to a cheese and reduce the waxiness that comes from shea. The saturated fat component is a combination of palmitic and stearic acids, both of which are considered better than lauric acid. As with the other hard fats, make sure that it is labeled refined or deodorized. Otherwise, your cheese and butter will end up tasting like chocolate!

COAGULANTS AND GELLING AGENTS

Just like dairy milk, plant milks need help to bind the proteins together and coagulate. In some cases, they need the aid of starches or natural gelling agents, such as the seaweed derivative, agar, to firm up. In this section, you'll learn about the various ingredients that lend body and consistency to plant milks.

Calcium sulfate, citric acid, lemon juice, or vinegar Animal milk is often coagulated using rennet, a natural enzyme found in the rumen of cows (although these days it is largely made through precision fermentation) or some plant derivatives, such as nettle, thistle, or artichoke. I have experimented unsuccessfully with plant-derived rennet in trying to coagulate plant milks. On the other hand, natural minerals such as calcium sulfate, or acidic ingredients such as citric acid, lemon juice, or vinegar, can do the trick quite well.

Starches Traditional animal milk has a magical protein profile that will lend viscosity and texture (such as stretchiness, attributable to casein) through coagulation. Plant milks don't function in the same way and sometimes need a little help from other members of the plant kingdom, such as tapioca, for texture and functionality. Most commercially available vegan cheeses are, sadly, just coagulated fats with lots of starch (and enhanced with "natural" flavors), which is why they will begin to dry out and crack within hours if left out of their package and exposed to air for an extended period.

In this book, starches are adjunct "helpers," but not the primary ingredient. The starches used in the recipes are tapioca, potato, and rice, along with psyllium husk powder, which is less processed and full of fiber. In many recipes, I have utilized ingredients that contain natural starch (such as the potato in Angel's Sharp Potato Cheddar, page 134), which naturally add to the texture of the recipe. Generally speaking, I have avoided the use of starches whenever possible.

Transglutaminase There is one other coagulant called transglutaminase, also known charmingly as "meat glue" because it binds proteins together. It is a natural enzyme found in animals (including humans) and plants. Today, vegan transglutaminase is available online at a handful of specialty shops but is definitely much pricier than alternatives, such as calcium sulfate. More than any other coagulant, it coagulates most milks in a way that resembles animal milks, yielding a solid mass that is then cut to release the whey, creating a curd with an incredibly smooth texture. It works better with higher protein milks, yielding a fairly firm curd. In my opinion, the results after aging or ripening aren't appreciably better than cheeses coagulated with just heat or other coagulants, however.

Agar-agar and carrageenan powder Both are seaweed derivatives that have gelling capabilities and can add texture or create hard cheeses. Their gelling properties are different, however, with agar producing a stiff, brittle gel, and carrageenan more elastic like gelatin. However, tapioca starch used in conjunction with agar can create a similar elastic texture to carrageenan. Both algae have been used for centuries in Asia, and carrageenan has also been used in Europe.

Agar-agar comes in both flake and powder form; it is very important that the powder form be used. Carrageenan is typically found only in powder form, although some natural food stores carry the red algae from which it is derived. For purposes of this book, it's important that only the powder forms of either be used. Specifically, for carrageenan, look for kappa carrageenan.

Agar-agar is activated fully only when it reaches close to a boiling temperature (around 208°F). Therefore, I generally cook it separately in water until it has fully melted before combining it with the other ingredients (carrageenan is activated at around 180°F).

Both agar and carrageenan are thermoreversible, which means that they will melt when heated, and thus, work for cheeses that require melting.

FLAVOR ENHANCERS

The following are all natural fermented ingredients that allow us to expand the variety of flavors. While not used for all, they can add depth and umami, or help some plant milks mimic more traditional animal cheeses. As plant-milk cheesemaking evolves over the years, we may discover different bacteria and microbes that work with plant milks to provide all the flavor and umami they need without the addition of anything but salt. For now, we take a middle road and utilize available tools.

Nutritional yeast flakes Nutritional yeast flakes (don't use the powder!), lovingly referred to as "nooch" by many vegans, is a deactivated yeast full of protein and vitamin B (including B_{12}), which adds cheesy goodness to many recipes. Many vegan cheese recipes rely on this for providing that cheesy flavor. It is critical in many recipes in this book. Make sure that your "nooch" is tasty enough to sprinkle on your popcorn or spaghetti before using it for your cheese, as some brands are not as tasty as others. Red Star and Bragg both make tasty nutritional yeast.

Miso This is a paste traditionally made from soybeans fermented with *kōji* (see below). More recently, nonsoy options of miso, made from other legumes, such as chickpeas, are available. Miso adds saltiness and a savory, cheesy flavor to plant-milk cheeses that develops over time. As a fermented food with live cultures, it also aids in the fermentation process. Choose a white (shiro) or light miso for this book.

Shio-kōji This is a mold—*Aspergillus oryzae*—that saccharifies rice and other grains, meaning that it converts starches into sugar, and eventually, alcohol. Kōji is also used to make miso, soy sauce, sake, and more. Kōji can add an amazing amount of umami to some cheeses, especially as they age. Fortunately, it has become more widely available, especially in natural foods or high-end grocery stores in the form of *shio-kōji* (salt kōji), a combination of the kōji mold with water and salt. This can be utilized in many culinary applications as well, from vegetables to tofu to mushrooms, and is used in a number of recipes in this book to add umami and aid fermentation.

EQUIPMENT

While a good, high-powered blender is essential for making most of the recipes in this book, let's remember that humans have been making creamery products for millennia without the fancy appliances we now have. For example, while yogurt makers exist today, I first learned to make yogurt (from cow's milk) forty-five years ago in Cairo from an Egyptian cook who literally wrapped the jar of warm milk in some towels and set it on a counter to ferment. If you have regular kitchen items, such as bowls, jars, sieves, and spoons, you'll be able to make most of the recipes in this book.

Blender

To achieve the best results, this is a necessary, not an optional, appliance. I highly recommend one of two brands: Vitamix or Blendtec. Either of these will do the trick in pureeing the toughest nuts and seeds, rendering them as smooth as possible, or emulsifying butter or cream.

What about the fancy almond milk makers now on the market? I have an Almond Cow myself and love it for making milk and cream—it's easier than the blender, as the machine strains the pulp itself (although very fine particulates can remain in the milk). However, the ratios of nuts or seeds to water required by the machines, as well as some other processes required for a recipe, may not make it a feasible option for many recipes in the book. I also find that the remaining pulp is very wet and have to use a nut milk bag to squeeze it in the end anyway.

Digital Scale and Measuring Cups and Spoons

Americans are accustomed to volumetric measurements using cups, tablespoons, and more, while the rest of the world uses the metric system, which measures by weight. I've provided measurements in both the US volumetric and metric systems, but I personally prefer the ease and accuracy of weighing things.

Proofing Box or Dehydrator

If you plan to make cheese or yogurt regularly, you may want to invest in a proofing box (such as is used for bread) or a dehydrator that will maintain a warm temperature between 80° and 120°F. Some ovens also have a low setting (90° to 100°F) that may work as well. Otherwise, you can rig something—such as finding a warm place or wrapping the container in a blanket or puffy jacket.

Ripening Boxes

If you are planning to make any mold-ripened cheeses, such as a blue or a bloomy rind, you will need to create a humid environment for mold growth. This can be accomplished by using a large food storage container with a lid that is big enough to hold your cheese, whether glass or plastic. This also helps to isolate cross-contamination in the event you have two different kinds of cheese ripening in your refrigerator, such as a blue and a Camembert. If you are planning to make large quantities, you can of course forgo containers and procure a wine fridge and dedicate it to a blue or a bloomy rind, but cross-contamination happens easily, so don't make them both in the same fridge.

Cheese Mats

For aging or ripening (see Ripening Boxes above), cheese needs air circulation. Placing the cheese on a mat, and then preferably on a little rack, allows for this. You can buy a cheese mat at one of the purveyors listed in the Resources (page 201) or use a plastic embroidery mat available at art stores. Cheese mats also ease flipping cheese, as you can place another one on top and flip easily. They can also add a beautiful imprint on the exterior of your cheese.

Cheesecloth and Nut Milk Bags

Whether you're just making milk or turning it into cheese, you will need either a cheesecloth or a nut milk bag to strain the pulp from the milk or the curds from the whey. I usually use 90-gauge cheesecloth and have nut milk bags in a variety of different sizes on hand.

Cheese Molds

Seriously, these can be anything from bowls to containers to loaf pans lined with plastic wrap; silicone baking molds work beautifully, too. For cheeses that need to drain, investing a few dollars in cheese molds that have holes can allow you to drain and shape your cheese all at once, but you can also just use a sieve or cheesecloth to drain, then form the cheese in a household container. Check online or in the Resources (page 201).

Cheese Wax

If you're old enough, you likely remember when certain cheeses were coated in a beautiful red wax. Wax is used to preserve the life of cheese, allowing it to continue to breathe and age while inhibiting mold growth. You can even keep waxed cheese at room temperature! Waxing a hard cheese is a way to extend shelf life and continue the aging process. I have made waxed cheeses and aged them for as long as three years, and I've been shocked at the changes to both flavor and texture when cheeses are allowed to "hibernate," developing complexity and often, a very traditional dairy-cheeselike texture that is pliable, waxy, and firm.

What is this wax made of? Traditionally, it was made of beeswax. Today, it's made of a food-grade paraffin, and must be removed prior to eating.

HOW TO WAX CHEESE

It's easy to wax cheese. Place a block of wax in a heavy pot and melt it over low heat to 160° to 170°F. Some people prefer to brush the wax onto the cheese using a pastry brush, but I prefer to dip one side at a time. It dries within seconds, so dip, wait for it to be hard enough to hold the waxed part, then dip the other side. You may need two coats, depending on how well you have coated it. Any openings will allow oxygen in, which encourages mold to grow, so make sure the entire surface is coated. As the wax in the pot cools, you'll need to reheat it briefly to remelt.

To clean the pot afterward, pour out any remaining wax into a parchment-lined container (for easy peeling later) and then heat the pot with water until boiling to remove any last residue. Pour this liquid through a sieve lined with a paper towel to catch the wax particles.

I have more recently seen liquid waxes available (thecheesemaker.com) that simply require dipping a brush in it and brushing it on the cheese. They also contain a substance called *natamycin,* a bacterium that is a mold inhibitor, which can help prevent mold from growing on your cheese (a crack in regular wax can lead to mold introduction). See the Resources section to see where you can get cheese wax.

pH Meter

A pH meter is a helpful tool if you plan to make cheese or other fermented items. You can also just rely on your taste buds to see if a cheese has fermented to your liking.

Digital Thermometer

A digital thermometer is a highly useful tool, as many of the recipes are temperature sensitive. This tool is not costly and will save you money in the long run trying to "guess" the temperature without doing an actual reading.

Humidity Meter

A digital humidity meter can be very helpful if you are going to make mold-ripened cheeses where knowing the ambient humidity is important. It is inexpensive and often features both the level of humidity and the ambient temperature, which can help you make sure you have your cheese in the right location.

CHAPTER I

In the Land of Milk and Cream

oday, half of US families have a plant milk in the fridge, and many say they simply prefer the taste over cow's milk. Plant milks now represent 15 percent of all US fluid milk sales. That's the fun thing about plant milks—oat, almond, soy, rice, pistachio—they're all different, and people can choose their favorite. When you bring the milk production in-house, meaning in *your* house, you can customize them even more!

Commercial nondairy milks typically take a single-ingredient approach—almond milk vs. oat milk vs. soy milk, focusing on one ingredient. This is where "purity" doesn't serve any purpose. Because some single-ingredient milks may lack a specific desirable attribute, producers often add adjuncts, such as sugar or oil or gums, to provide that extra richness or mouthfeel, while adding no nutritional benefit. However, if we combine some of these base ingredients—almonds with oats for extra mouthfeel, for example, or oats with hemp hearts to double the protein—we can avoid the extraneous adjuncts and create delicious, more balanced milks in both flavor and nutrition. That's what I've tried to do here—to combine complementary ingredients to boost flavor or nutrition.

You'll find milk to pour on your cereal, a "barista" version that creates supple foam for your cappuccino, and others that perform like heavy cream to thicken soups and sauces. And with so many allergies going around, I've tried to cover the bases with the variety of ingredients!

Milking plants is certainly easier than milking a cow and certainly more compassionate. All you need is a blender and a nut milk bag for filtering. If you want to splurge on a plant-milk machine, go ahead, but you may have to adjust the manufacturer's recommended ratios to make these recipes work.

CREAMY ALMOND-OAT MILK

MAKES ABOUT 4½ CUPS (1.1L)

1 cup (140g) almonds (if not using a high-powered blender, soak for 8 hours in cold water or 1 hour in hot water, then drain)

4 cups (950ml) water

⅓ cup (30g) rolled oats

1 teaspoon maple syrup (optional)

Pinch of fine sea salt

Almond and oat milk compete for the top spot among consumers, even though it's well known that most commercial almond milks are mainly water with just a few almonds per carton. By combining both oats and almonds we can create a milk that is rich and creamy!

Almond milk dates back millennia to the Middle East, where it was frequently used in recipes, then made its way to Europe during medieval times, where it was consumed during Lent and used for medicinal purposes, purportedly curing coughs. Hundreds of years later, it's made it to the tables of millions of Americans as the top alternative milk.

IN A BLENDER, combine the almonds, water, oats, maple syrup (if using), and salt and process on high until smooth, 1 minute or longer. Pour the mixture through a nut milk bag or a sieve lined with cheesecloth into a bowl and squeeze as much milk out as possible. (Reserve the pulp for another use; see Note.) Store in a clean jar or container in the refrigerator for up to 1 week.

NOTE

Reserve the pulp to make something delicious, such as the No-Waste Crackers (page 189).

FORTIFIED OAT MILK

MAKES ABOUT 4½ CUPS (1.1L)

⅔ cup (70g) rolled oats
(see Note)

4 cups (950ml) water

¼ cup (35g) hemp hearts

2 teaspoons maple syrup
(optional)

Pinch of fine sea salt

Despite the hype, commercial oat milks often derive their creaminess from added oil because oats are so low in fat. Oat milks also tend to be low in protein. By adding just an ounce of hemp hearts, we can not only double the protein to 5 grams per serving but also enhance richness, making it perfect for morning cereal as well as in a creamy soup. This oat milk also foams nicely for your cappuccino, although the hemp flavor is more pronounced when heated.

IN A BLENDER, combine the oats, water, hemp hearts, maple syrup (if using), and the salt and process until smooth, 1 minute or longer. Pour the mixture through a nut milk bag or a sieve lined with cheesecloth and squeeze out the milk, stopping when it begins to feel sludgy. Store in a clean container or jar in the refrigerator for up to 1 week.

NOTE

Some people find that their homemade oat milk can be a little slimy. To reduce this effect, the oats can be soaked briefly in water before processing. Simply cover the oats with water and let them soak for at least 10 minutes. Stir this around and then drain through a sieve, then rinse them under running water for a minute or two (this further eliminates any hint of sliminess).

BARLEY MILK

MAKES ABOUT 5 CUPS (1.2L)

1 cup (148g) hulled barley

6 cups (1.4L) water

2 teaspoons maple syrup

Pinch of fine sea salt

Like oat milk, barley milk has a light, creamy texture and neutral flavor that can be enhanced with just a teaspoon or two of maple syrup. The fun thing about this milk is that the "sludge" that results from straining the milk can be cooked into a "cream of barley" cereal (below) similar to Cream of Wheat that's wonderful for breakfast with fruit and—well, barley milk!

Due to the residual starch, barley milk thickens when heated. Therefore, you'll need to make sure that you stir it with a whisk to prevent clumping when used as a cream to thicken soups and sauces.

IN A LARGE glass jar or bowl, combine the barley with water to cover by at least 2 inches. Let it soak for at least 8 hours or overnight. Drain the barley in a sieve and rinse well. Save the sludge to make Cream of Barley Cereal.

In a blender, combine the barley and 6 cups (1.4L) water and blend until smooth and creamy. Pour the mixture through a nut milk bag and squeeze, being sure to stop squeezing when the milk starts to get gooey; what remains in the bag should be a gooey sludge.

Stir in the maple syrup and salt. Store in a clean container in the refrigerator for up to 1 week.

Cream of Barley Cereal

MAKES 1 OR 2 SERVINGS

Barley "sludge" from 1 batch Barley Milk

½ cup (120ml) water or barley milk

This takes me back to my childhood when I first came to the United States and ate Cream of Wheat for breakfast instead of rice. I didn't like oatmeal at first, but Cream of Wheat quickly grew on me. After making the barley milk, the "sludge" can be refrigerated for a day or two before making the cereal, or you can cook it right away and reheat it later when you're ready to eat the cereal.

IN A SMALL saucepan, combine the barley sludge and water and whisk well. Bring to a simmer over low heat until it thickens, thinning it out with more water or milk as necessary. Serve hot.

CASHEW MILK AND CREAM

MAKES 1 QUART (1L)

1 cup (140g) cashews (if not using a high-powered blender, soak in water to cover for 3 to 4 hours, then drain and rinse)

5 cups (1.2L) water

1 teaspoon vanilla extract (optional)

2 pitted dates, or 2 teaspoons maple syrup (optional)

Cashew milk is the simplest of all milks to make because it requires no soaking or straining—just a decent whir in your high-powered blender, and a delicious, rich milk results. Because cashews are high in starch, the milk will thicken when heated—a wonderful substitute for heavy cream (which also thickens) in making soups and sauces.

IN A BLENDER, combine the cashews, water, vanilla (if using), and dates or maple syrup (if using) and process on high until smooth and creamy, about 1 minute. There is no need to strain cashew milk if you've used a high-powered blender; you may want to strain through a nut milk bag if you've used a regular blender just to ensure smoothness and remove any chalkiness. For ultrasmooth milk or cream even with a high-powered blender, you may want to strain it to remove any hint of chalkiness (depending on how sensitive you are to this). Store in a glass jar in the refrigerator for up to 10 days.

Cashew Cream

MAKES 3 CUPS (710ML)

Cashew cream is a terrific substitute for heavy cream in cooking or for coffee creamer. It will thicken up quite a bit when heated, achieving a texture akin to white sauce or béchamel sauce. Hence, it's an excellent addition to creamy soups or creamy pasta sauces, and can be pureed with garlic, herbs, or other seasonings.

FOLLOW THE DIRECTIONS for Cashew Milk, but reduce the water to 3 cups (710ml), a 1 to 3 ratio of cashews to water. For use in a savory application (such as a soup), omit the vanilla and sweetener. For use as a coffee creamer, adding the vanilla and sweetener is still optional. Store in a jar in the refrigerator for 1 to 2 weeks.

LUCKY PUMPKIN SEED MILK

MAKES 1 QUART (1L)

1 cup (140g) pumpkin seeds
(if not using a high-powered
blender, soak in water for 4 to
6 hours, then drain and rinse)

3½ cups (830ml) water

1 teaspoon maple syrup

Pinch of fine sea salt

With a pale hint of green, this lovely milk is neutral in taste and contains around 7 grams of protein per cup. For drinking and using on cereal, this could be your lucky milk! Note, however, that it can curdle if heated too high, so don't use it for cooking. And be sure to try the cheesy crisps (below) from the residual pulp!

IN A BLENDER, combine the pumpkin seeds, water, maple syrup, and salt and process on high speed until creamy, about 1 minute. Pour the mixture through a nut milk bag and squeeze to extract as much milk as possible. (Reserve the pulp for another use; see Note.) Store in a glass container in the refrigerator for up to 1 week.

(NOTE)

See the recipes in No-Waste Recipes and Other Favorites chapter on pages 183 to 199.

Gluten-Free Cheesy Crisps

MAKES 18 TO 24 CRISPS

Pulp from 1 batch Lucky
Pumpkin Seed Milk (above)

6 tablespoons nutritional
yeast flakes

¼ cup (80ml) olive brine

2 tablespoons extra-virgin
olive oil

½ teaspoon fine sea salt

This comes together quickly and is a light, crunchy, tasty snack to have with your milk.

PREHEAT THE OVEN to 350°F.

In a bowl, stir together the pulp, nutritional yeast, brine, olive oil, and sea salt until it is uniform in color. It should be like a paste. Roll this out between two sheets of parchment (or you can just pat it out with your hands) until it is about ⅛ inch (3mm) thick, like a thick cracker. Transfer this (between the two sheets) to a sheet pan, then peel off the top sheet of parchment paper. Using a sharp knife, cut the dough into 18 to 24 rectangles.

Bake until browned and crispy, 15 to 20 minutes.

Let them cool on the pan, then store in an airtight container in the refrigerator to prevent them from getting moist and soft.

HAZELNUT MILK AND CREAMER

MAKES ABOUT 3½ CUPS (830ML)

4 cups (950ml) water

1½ cups (180g) unsalted roasted hazelnuts

1 tablespoon maple syrup or organic sugar

1 teaspoon vanilla extract

Unabashedly nutty while being rich and delicious, hazelnut milk is a flavorful drink that also makes an indulgent creamer. And, oh, did I mention hot chocolate? Well, this is the milk for that. Raw hazelnuts will make a lovely milk with a subtle nutty flavor, while toasted will make it really nutty—it's up to you which you choose.

IN A BLENDER, combine the water and hazelnuts and process on high until smooth and creamy, 1 to 2 minutes. Pour this mixture through a nut milk bag and squeeze to extract as much milk as possible. Pour into a 1-quart (1L) jar, add the maple syrup and vanilla, and shake well. (Reserve the pulp for another use; see Note.) Store in the refrigerator for up to 1 week.

 NOTE

Save the pulp to make Luscious Gluten-Free Salted Hazelnut Brownies (page 198).

Hazelnut Creamer

MAKES 2½ CUPS (600ML)

This is a little richer than the hazelnut milk, making it perfect as a creamer for your coffee.

FOLLOW THE DIRECTIONS for Hazelnut Milk, but reduce the water to 2 cups (470ml) and reduce the hazelnuts to 1 cup (120g). Store in the refrigerator for 1 to 2 weeks.

MELON SEED MILK

MAKES A GENEROUS 3 CUPS (750ML)

3 cups (710ml) water

About 1 cup (100g to 140g) melon seeds, scraped out of any melon

1 tablespoon sweetener of choice: monk fruit, coconut sugar, organic sugar, or 2 dates

Ever wonder if you could do anything with all the melon seeds you scrape out of your cantaloupe or honeydew at the height of the season? Well, make milk! You needn't even wash the seeds to rid them of the melon-y strands—they can be incorporated to add flavor and color. The seeds themselves are high in protein and have a delicate flavor; with a dash of sweetener, whether evil sugar or a healthier date, it's a milk that's fit for cereal, smoothies, or just as a refreshing beverage with a hint of melon flavor. So next time you cut into a cantaloupe, turn the seeds into milk! You can make a small amount from one melon, or save and freeze them in a bag until you've accumulated at least 1 cup for a full recipe.

IN A BLENDER, combine the water, seeds (and strands), and sweetener and process on high speed until smooth and creamy. Pour the mixture into a nut milk bag and squeeze to extract the milk—there should not be a lot of pulp left, as the seeds are fairly soft. Store in a glass jar or container in the refrigerator for 3 to 4 days.

NOTE

If you prefer a pure white milk without any melon flavor, rinse the seeds well in a colander. Otherwise, just measure with the melon strands and goop included, and enjoy a sweet and delicious melon-flavored milk!

WATERMELON SEED KERNEL MILK AND CREAMER

**MAKES A GENEROUS
4 CUPS (1L)**

1½ cups (210g) watermelon seed kernels (see Resources, page 201)

4 cups (950ml) water

1 tablespoon sweetener of choice: maple syrup, coconut sugar, organic sugar, or 2 dates

Pinch of sea salt

No, you're not going to spit out little black seeds from your summer watermelon and save them to make a glass of milk. These little white seeds are a popular snack in places like China and India and come from a variety of melons grown for their seeds. High in protein and neutral in flavor, they produce a beautiful, rich-tasting milk with a mouthfeel that rivals cow's milk, either cold or heated and foamed for a coffee drink. Be careful: This milk tolerates only a certain degree of heat before it coagulates. So you can heat it in a foamer, but don't try to simmer or boil it.

IN A BLENDER, process the watermelon seed kernels on high speed for a minute to produce a cornmeal-like flour. Add the water, sweetener, and salt and process until creamy, about a minute. Pour the mixture into a nut milk bag and squeeze to extract the milk. Store in a glass jar in the refrigerator for 5 to 7 days.

> **NOTE**

Although this produces very little pulp compared with other seeds, you can reserve it and check the recipes in the No-Waste Recipes and Other Favorites chapter on pages 183 to 199.

Watermelon Seed Kernel Creamer

**MAKES ABOUT 3 CUPS
(700ML)**

Follow the directions for Watermelon Seed Kernel Milk, but reduce the water to 3 cups (700ml). Store in a glass jar in the refrigerator for 5 to 7 days.

BARISTA-STYLE MILKS AND CREAMERS

More and more people have fancy espresso machines and want milks that foam. Soy milk is the only commercial milk that naturally foams without a bunch of stuff added to it; almond, oat, and other "barista-style" milks gain their foaming property from the addition of oils and stabilizers. I wanted to find a way to make a healthy option at home without those things and so tested every milk I made for this functionality. Some milks naturally foam better than others, but was there an ingredient that could be added to nonfoaming milks to get them to foam? Yes! That discovery was sunflower seeds! In this section, we explore milks that naturally foam, and include a few more made with the addition of sunflower seeds.

Sunflower Seed Milk

MAKES 4 CUPS (950ML)

3½ cups (846ml) water

¾ cup (100g) sunflower seeds

Pinch of sea salt

1 tablespoon maple syrup
(optional)

2 teaspoons vanilla extract
(optional)

This is what kicked off my exploration to make the best foaming milk. It's delicious to drink and just fabulous foamed hot or cold. For a cold latte or cappuccino, you can even foam it in your blender.

IN A BLENDER, combine the water, sunflower seeds, salt, maple syrup (if using), and vanilla extract (if using) and blend on high speed until smooth and creamy, about 1 minute. Pour the mixture into a nut milk bag and squeeze to extract the milk. (Reserve the pulp for another use; see Note.) Store in a clean jar or container in the refrigerator for 1 week.

NOTE

Save the pulp, which is very soft, and season with salt and spices to use as a spread for sandwiches.

CONTINUED

Rich and Refreshing Soy Milk

**MAKES A GENEROUS
4 CUPS (1L)**

1½ cups (255g) organic dried
soybeans, preferably small

6 cups (1.4L) water

Pinch of fine sea salt

1 tablespoon maple syrup
(optional)

1 teaspoon vanilla extract
(optional)

I did "blind taste tests" on friends and family of different soy
milks I'd made and confirmed that this unorthodox method
created the most neutral tasting, refreshing milk without an
overpowering beany flavor. What's the secret? Don't soak the
beans in cold water. I came up with this method when I began
to wonder why commercial soy milks didn't taste as beany as
homemade ones, and I learned that the enzyme responsible for
the beany flavor is activated when exposed to cold water. By
skipping this soaking step and boiling the dried beans as the
first step, we can make a soy milk that's refreshing and neutral
in flavor and foams beautifully for your morning latte.

A note about the beans themselves: Choose non-GMO or
organic soybeans from the most recent harvest, and if possible,
get the smaller ones grown for *natto*—these generally taste
better.

BRING A LARGE pot of water to a boil. Add the soybeans and boil for
10 minutes. Turn off the heat and let the beans sit in the hot water
for at least 1 and up to 4 hours. Drain and rinse the beans.

In a blender, add half the beans and 3 cups (710ml) water and process
on high speed for about a minute. Pour the mixture into a nut milk bag
and squeeze to extract as much milk as possible into a large pot (the
same one you used for boiling the beans). Repeat with the remaining
soybeans and 3 cups (710ml) water. (Reserve the pulp for another use;
see Notes.)

Bring the milk to a boil. Reduce the heat to a rapid simmer, cover, and
cook for 30 minutes. Make sure it doesn't boil over. The lid will prevent
rapid evaporation of the soy milk as well as the formation of a skin
(called yuba). Measure the milk after 30 minutes to see if it has reduced
to about 1 quart (1L); if not, cook a bit longer. Let the milk cool. If using
maple syrup and/or vanilla, stir them in. Store in a large jar or container
in the refrigerator for up to 1 week.

NOTES

*I usually double or triple
the batch, since the work is
the same and I don't have to
repeat it again a few days
later.*

*Reserve the pulp, known
as okara, for another use,
such as No-Waste Italian
Sausages and Sausage
Crumbles with Okara
(page 187).*

Almond and Sunflower Seed Creamer

MAKES 2 CUPS (470ML)

2 cups (470ml) water

⅔ cup (90g) almonds (if not using a high-powered blender, soak for 8 hours in cold water, then drain and rinse)

Generous ⅓ cup (50g) sunflower seeds

1 tablespoon maple syrup or organic sugar (optional)

Almond milk gets a little help from sunflower seeds to turn into a rich creamer with a beautiful rich foam.

IN A BLENDER, combine the water, almonds, and sunflower seeds and process on high speed until creamy and smooth. Strain through a nut milk bag. Stir in the optional sweetener if desired. Store in a glass jar in the refrigerator for up to 1 week.

Noncurdling Creamer

MAKES 2 CUPS (470ML)

½ cup (70g) cashews

⅓ cup (60g) sunflower seeds

2 cups (470ml) water

¼ cup (60ml) aquafaba (chickpea water)

1 tablespoon maple syrup or organic sugar

1 teaspoon vanilla extract (optional)

Pinch of fine sea salt

Ever have your coffee creamer curdle in your coffee? I hate that. When the proteins in the creamer hit the hot liquid, they separate and curdle. I love my cashew creamer but have struggled with this problem. Combining it with sunflower seeds and aquafaba seems to minimize it, creating a rich and creamy creamer, which, in my testing, curdles less than other milks.

IN A BLENDER, combine the cashews, sunflower seeds, water, aquafaba, sweetener, vanilla (if using), and salt and process on high speed until creamy, 1 to 2 minutes. Pour the mixture into a nut milk bag and squeeze to extract as much milk as possible. (Reserve the pulp for another use; see Note.) Store in a jar in the refrigerator for 7 to 10 days.

NOTE

The pulp is very soft and can be mixed into a hot cereal such as oatmeal or Cream of Barley Cereal (page 46).

SWEET WHIPPING CREAM AND TOPPING

MAKES A GENEROUS 2 CUPS (500ML)

1 cup (240ml) soy milk (homemade, page 58, or store-bought), Watermelon Seed Kernel Milk (page 54), or water

½ cup (110g) refined coconut oil, melted

¼ cup (35g) cashews

¼ cup (50g) organic sugar

1 teaspoon vanilla extract

This is a soft, fluffy, light-as-air whipped cream that's perfect for topping pies, berries, and sundaes. I like to make several batches of this—it's easy to double the batch in a blender. You can make this whipping cream ahead and keep some on hand in the freezer to whip up whenever the mood strikes. Using soy milk or Watermelon Seed Kernel Milk will mimic whipped cream, whereas water will make it similar to a frozen whipped topping such as Cool Whip. Take your pick and make a grand dessert!

IN A BLENDER, combine the soy milk, coconut oil, cashews, sugar, and vanilla and puree until smooth. Pour into a covered container and freeze overnight (or as long as you like).

When you are ready to whip, take it out of the freezer and let it sit on the counter for 30 minutes or so to soften slightly. In a bowl, with an electric mixer, whip until it forms soft or stiff peaks, 5 to 8 minutes. If you overwhip, it could curdle and separate, so pay attention if you are using a stand mixer.

Once the cream is whipped, it's best to decorate your cake or dessert as soon as possible. The cream will firm up if refrigerated. If you want it to be fluffy and creamy, rewhip it very briefly.

CHAPTER 2

Butter, Sour Cream, Spreads

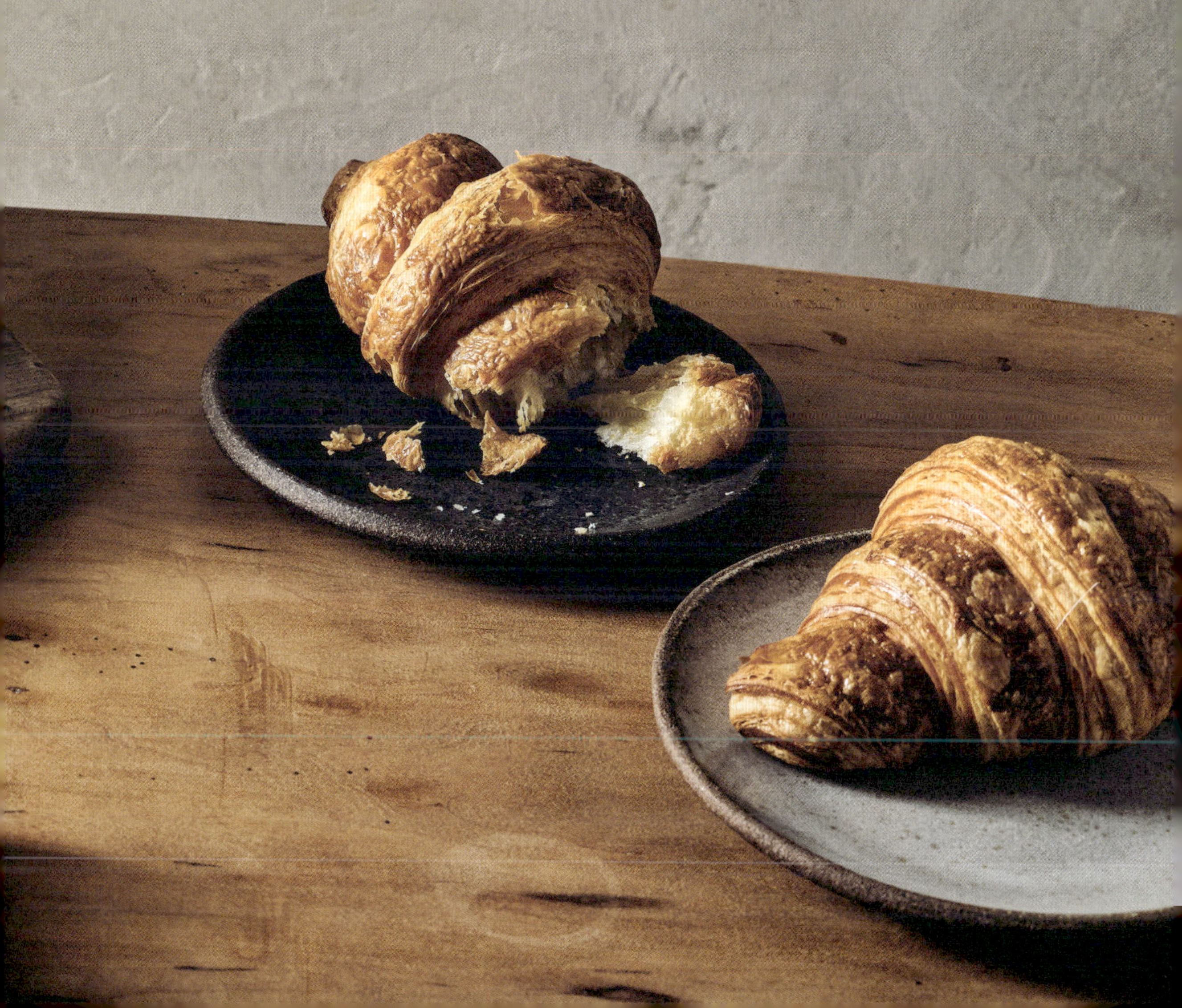

Before I went from vegetarian to vegan in the 1980s, I worked my way through every vegetarian recipe in Julia Child's *Mastering the Art of French Cooking* to learn how to melt, clarify, whip, and *add* copious amounts of butter and heavy cream to practically everything, infusing dishes with flavor and incomparable richness. You could say that my motto was: "When in doubt, just add more butter."

My approach to cooking is a bit lighter now, and while I might on occasion enjoy a generous dose of butter on a warm baguette or baked in a flaky croissant, most days I prefer simpler, less-rich foods. Still, I can't deny that on special occasions, nothing spruces up your culinary game better than butter, sour cream, or crème fraîche. Unfortunately, a lot of commercially available vegan alternatives for these are made with cheap oils, unnatural flavors, and who knows what. I hope the recipes offered in this chapter help elevate your culinary game, adding an artisan touch, whether you're dining alone or entertaining a crowd.

SOFT SPREADABLE BUTTER

MAKES ABOUT 2 TO 3 CUPS (450 TO 600G) (DEPENDING ON THE AMOUNT OF MILK USED)

¾ cup (157g) melted, refined coconut oil

1 cup (196g) avocado or other liquid oil of choice

½ to 1 cup (120 to 240ml) cold nondairy milk (homemade—do not use store-bought milk except soy) or yogurt, such as soy, cashew, or watermelon seed kernel milk

¼ to ½ teaspoon fine sea salt, to taste

1 to 2 drops liquid annatto for color (optional)

We've all heard that water and oil don't mix, but that's exactly what buttery spreads are. The key to combining the two is usually an emulsifier, lecithin. Here, it's the order of ingredients that somehow magically emulsifies it. This is the technique I used to make mayonnaise, and one day I thought to apply the same technique to make butter. And voilà! It worked. Note that there is a range on the amount of milk you can add—the more milk, the softer the spread.

This butter is soft and spreadable right out of the fridge. You can use it for some baked goods, such as muffins or other soft items, but opt for the Baking and Culinary Butter (page 70) for flaky pastries such as puff pastry.

IN A BLENDER or the jar used for an immersion blender, combine the coconut oil and liquid oil, and process on medium for about 15 seconds until cloudy and white. (If it does not turn cloudy and white, it is likely too warm. Place the jar in the refrigerator and let it chill until it is around or below 80°F.) Pour in the cold milk or yogurt in a steady stream, add the salt and optional annatto, and continue blending. Within 15 to 20 seconds, it will start to thicken and look like mayonnaise. The more milk you add, the thicker it will become (the blender blades may even stop turning) and the softer it will be for spreading after chilling. Transfer the mixture into a container and chill.

If the mixture does not thicken into a mayonnaise-type texture in the blender, the temperature was too high. Place the jar in the refrigerator for 30 minutes, then reprocess.

Store in the refrigerator for 3 to 4 weeks, or in the freezer for many months.

COMPOUND BUTTERS

A compound butter is a flavored butter, either sweet or savory, and can be made with any of the butters in this book. Note that the final texture will depend on which butter you use, so if you want a spreadable one, use the Soft Spreadable Butter (page 66); if you want a sticklike result, use the Baking and Culinary Butter (page 70). The following flavor additions are for one-third to one-quarter of a batch of butter, give or take—you likely won't want to make a huge batch of a compound butter. You can feel free to adjust the seasonings to your liking. I will often make a batch of one of my butters, then divide into 3 or 4 portions and flavor each differently just to have some fun and tasty spreads. Let your imagination run wild with different flavor combinations, using these simply as a starting point. Another suggestion: Make these right after the butter comes out of the blender as a thick cream *before* you refrigerate it to firm up—mixing in the ingredients is much simpler this way! If you're going to make them from a batch of cold, hardened butter, let it come to room temperature first to make stirring in additions easier.

Cinnamon Maple Butter

To about one-quarter of any of the butter recipes, add 1 tablespoon maple syrup, a couple of dashes of ground cinnamon, and ½ teaspoon vanilla extract and stir well with a spoon. Adjust seasoning to taste. Great on morning toast!

Flower Power Butter

This one is just so pretty—perfect for a special spring occasion when you want to impress. Make this in the blender. To about one-quarter of any of the butter recipes, add 1 tablespoon sugar, 1 teaspoon vanilla extract, and a small handful of edible flower petals, such as marigolds, pansies, violets, or nasturtiums (edible flowers can be gathered or are often sold in packets in the produce section). Blitz very briefly to break the petals down so you have butter with a colorful, confetti-like appearance. Pretty on scones or pancakes!

Truffle Butter

To about one-quarter of any of the butter recipes, stir in ½ to 1 teaspoon good-quality truffle oil. If a little texture is desired, mince and sauté a few tablespoons of mushrooms (cremini or button), allow to cool completely, then stir them into the butter.

Cheesy Garlic Butter

Easy garlic toast! To about one-quarter of any of the butter recipes, stir in 2 or 3 minced garlic cloves, 2 tablespoons nutritional yeast flakes, and 1 tablespoon finely chopped fresh parsley.

Lemon Shallot Herb Butter

Lovely on potatoes, asparagus, pasta, rice, or more. To about one-quarter of any of the butter recipes, stir in 2 tablespoons sautéed minced shallots, 2 teaspoons chopped fresh thyme or tarragon, and a grating or two of fresh lemon zest.

BAKING AND CULINARY BUTTER (82% FAT)

MAKES 18 OUNCES (500G)

¾ cup (145g) refined coconut oil, melted and cooled to 80° to 90°F

¾ cup (145g) refined shea butter, melted and cooled to 80° to 90°F

½ cup (100g) cashew, avocado, or other liquid oil

½ cup (120ml) unsweetened nondairy yogurt or milk, cold from the fridge

½ teaspoon fine sea salt (or omit for unsalted butter)

1 to 2 drops liquid annatto for color (optional)

Traditional animal dairy butter hovers around 82% butterfat, while most plant-milk butters and margarines contain between 60% and 79% fat, depending on how soft they are. They are typically simple concoctions of oil and water that contain no type of plant milk at all, which means they do not brown (it's the milk solids that brown). When melted in a skillet, they sometimes just splatter as the water separates from the oil, unlike butter, which will brown and caramelize into a browned butter glory.

I wanted to create a butter with a fat content and melting curve similar to dairy butter to replicate its performance in baking and cooking. The combination of shea butter—which melts slowly, "lingering" in your mouth—with the faster-melting coconut oil creates a melting curve similar to dairy butter. The milk, of course, helps it to brown in a pan (do you miss browned butter?!). Use this to make the flakiest croissants and buttery scones or for browned butter sauces.

IN A BLENDER jar or the jar used for an immersion blender, combine the coconut oil, shea butter, and liquid oil, and process on medium for about 15 seconds until cloudy and white. (If it does not turn cloudy and white, check the temperature—it is likely too warm. Place the jar in the refrigerator and let it chill until it is around or below 80°F.) Pour in the cold milk or yogurt in a steady stream, add the salt and optional annatto, and continue blending for 15 to 20 seconds, until it starts to thicken and look like mayonnaise. Transfer the mixture into a storage container and chill. (Alternatively, you can use a silicone butter mold for easy removal.)

If the mixture does not thicken into a mayonnaise-type texture in the blender, the temperature was too high. Place the jar in the refrigerator for 30 minutes, then reprocess.

Store in the refrigerator for 3 to 4 weeks, or in the freezer for many months.

Vegan Ghee

Ghee, or clarified butter, is made by heating butter to remove the milk solids, which in this case, would be the yogurt or milk. You can't make ghee from most commercial vegan butters because they are made by emulsifying only water with oil. The heating of the butter separates the milk solids and turns them nutty brown, making the clear oil highly flavorful.

TO MAKE GHEE, put 8 ounces (225g) of Baking and Culinary Butter (page 70) in a saucepan over low heat to melt, stirring occasionally. As it gets hot, it should start to foam. The foam will first be very big and then settle down to a fine consistency. After 3 to 5 minutes, the foam will subside, and the butter will be very clear with nutty brown particles on the bottom. Turn off the heat.

Set a fine-mesh sieve over a jar and slowly and carefully pour the ghee through the sieve to catch any brown particles. Let cool. Ghee does not need to be refrigerated as the milk particles have been removed, although refrigeration will extend shelf life even more. Store the ghee in a dark place for up to 2 months, or in the fridge for even longer.

SPREADABLE EVERYDAY OLIVE AND SHEA BUTTER

MAKES ABOUT 18 OUNCES (500G)

¾ cup (145g) melted, refined shea butter

¾ cup (160g) extra-virgin olive oil

¾ cup (187g) nondairy yogurt or plant milk, homemade or store-bought (see Note)

¾ teaspoon fine sea salt

1 to 2 drops liquid annatto for color (optional)

I'm not a doctor, but there's published research that coconut oil can raise the cholesterol of some people. The primary fatty acid in coconut oil is lauric acid, which apparently is the culprit. Shea butter's primary fatty acid is stearic, which is supposedly less harmful in terms of cholesterol. Combined with a high ratio of monounsaturated extra-virgin olive oil, considered a healthy fat, this may yet be the healthiest butter choice in this book—but let's remember that it's still an oil! This has become my go-to everyday butter.

Olive oil can impart a strong flavor, so select one that is on the milder side.

IF YOU ARE weighing the shea butter, put half in a small pot and melt over low heat. If you are using volumetric measurements, simply eyeball about half—it doesn't have to be exact. Remove from the heat and stir in the remaining shea butter until melted (this keeps the shea butter from getting too hot). If you have used volumetric measurements, pour the melted oil into a 1-cup measuring cup to ensure you have the right amount.

In a blender or the jar of an immersion blender, combine the melted shea butter and olive oil and process for about 15 seconds until cloudy and white. Add the milk in a steady stream until it thickens like mayonnaise. Add the salt and optional annatto and blend for another few seconds. If it doesn't thicken, place the jar in the refrigerator for about 30 minutes, then reblend until creamy and thick.

Transfer to the refrigerator, where it will get harder, although it will remain spreadable even when cold. Store in the refrigerator for 2 to 3 weeks, or in the freezer for several months.

NOTE

Don't use any commercial milk that is mostly water, such as commercial almond milk. Store-bought soy milk is okay, though.

FORMAGGIO FORTE SPREAD

MAKES ABOUT 18 OUNCES (500G)

1 pound (450g) various scraps of cheese (preferably half hard cheese, half soft cheese)

6 garlic cloves, peeled but whole

¼ to ½ cup (60ml to 120ml) white or red wine

Fine sea salt

If you start a cheesemaking journey, you'll likely end up with odd bits and remnants of cheese that are no longer suitable for a cheese board. Here's how you can transform those scraps that have seen better days into an all-new cheese that's delicious and powerful in flavor—hence the "forte." Serve with bread or crackers.

CHOP UP THE hard cheeses into small pieces about ½ inch in size. In a food processor, combine the hard cheese pieces and the garlic and process to chop and blend. Depending on how much of the hard cheese you have, as well as how hard it is, it may just reduce to crumbs or clump into a ball. Add the soft cheeses and process again until it starts to become creamed. Slowly add enough wine to process the cheese mixture into a spreadable consistency. Add salt to taste. Store in a covered container in the refrigerator for 3 to 4 weeks.

Holiday Cheese Ball

Omit the garlic and wine. Add ⅓ cup of nutritional yeast and 2 to 3 tablespoons of port wine, then process the cheese until mostly smooth. Form into a ball with your hands and roll in toasted, chopped walnuts, pecans, or almonds.

Ale to the Cheese

Reduce the garlic to 2 cloves. Instead of wine, use a good, strong ale of choice, and stir in ½ cup minced green onions or chives.

Variations

Feel free to skip the alcohol and just process with water. For a Mediterranean flair, add some olive oil–soaked sundried tomatoes and a few pitted kalamata olives. Use your imagination and change up the flavors!

LOVELY SOUR CREAM AND CRÈME FRAÎCHE

**MAKES 1 TO 1½ CUPS
(250G TO 375G)**

3 cups (710ml) water

1 cup (140g) almonds

3 tablespoons hemp hearts

1 tablespoon fresh lemon juice

½ teaspoon calcium sulfate

¼ teaspoon citric acid

⅛ teaspoon MinusMilk (vegan version of Flora Danica; see Resources, page 201) or other vegan mesophilic culture

This version of sour cream is light, rich, silky smooth, and creamy, and actually healthy—not just coagulated oil with some "gums" thrown in such as many commercial products, or a compromise made of pureed tofu or cashews with lemon juice.

IN A BLENDER, combine the water, almonds, and hemp hearts and process at high speed until smooth and creamy, 1 to 2 minutes. Pour the mixture into a nut milk bag and squeeze to extract the milk into a saucepan. (Reserve the pulp for another use; see pages 183 to 199.)

Set the saucepan over medium-low heat and heat the milk to 180°F, stirring occasionally with a silicone spatula to scrape the bottom and sides. Whisk in the lemon juice, calcium sulfate, and citric acid, dissolving the latter well. Allow the mixture to cool to between 80° and 90°F.

Stir in the MinusMilk and transfer to a sterilized jar or container with a lid. Place the jar in a warm place that will maintain a temperature of 85° to 90°F for 16 to 24 hours. Aim for a pH of around 4.5.

When it is ready, the mixture will be thick like yogurt, although there will likely be some separation. Pour the mixture through a nut milk bag and let it drain for about 1 hour. You should have about 1½ cups.

Transfer to a jar or container with a lid and store in the refrigerator where it will continue to thicken. Store in the refrigerator for 2 to 3 weeks but not in the freezer.

Crème Fraîche

The French cousin of American sour cream is richer, thicker, less acidic, and incredibly buttery.

FOLLOW THE SOUR Cream recipe but omit the citric acid. Aim for a slightly higher pH, around 4.8 to 5.0. On the second day, drain for 4 to 5 hours until you have 1 to 1¼ cups left. It will continue to thicken in the refrigerator. Store in the refrigerator for 2 to 3 weeks.

COCONUT CHICKPEA LABNEH

MAKES ABOUT 2 CUPS (450G)

8 ounces (225g) dried chickpeas, soaked overnight in water

3 cups (710ml) water

1 cup (225ml) full-fat coconut milk or coconut cream

¼ teaspoon vegan yogurt culture, such as Vegurt, or 3 tablespoons nondairy yogurt, homemade or store-bought

1 teaspoon sea salt

Optional add-ins: chopped fresh mint, za'atar, sesame seeds, garlic, or other seasoning of choice

Labneh is a creamy, cheesy Middle Eastern dip that is made simply by draining yogurt to remove the whey. What results is a tangy dip or spread that's slightly lighter than cream cheese and can be dressed up with seasonings such as za'atar, mint, fennel seeds, garlic, or whatever you dream up. This version is based on chickpeas but adds coconut cream for some richness and flavor.

You'll first make yogurt, which can be enjoyed on its own, then drain it to make this delicious spread.

DRAIN AND RINSE the soaked chickpeas well.

In a blender, combine the chickpeas, water, and coconut milk and process on high speed until smooth and creamy, about 1 minute. Pour the mixture into a nut milk bag and squeeze to extract as much milk as possible into a medium saucepan. (Reserve the pulp for another use; see pages 183 to 199.)

Set the saucepan over medium heat and cook until the mixture is very thick, whisking almost constantly and frequently scraping the bottom and sides with a silicone spatula. Pour this mixture into a 1-quart (1L) sterilized glass jar or container and allow it to cool in the refrigerator, stirring occasionally with a sterilized spoon, until it falls to about 110°F.

Stir in the culture or yogurt, cover with a lid, and set the jar in a warm place where it will maintain a temperature of 95° to 110°F for 8 to 16 hours, until it is as tangy as you like.

Drain the yogurt. You can do this by pouring it into a clean nut milk bag and hanging it from the sink for 12 to 24 hours, or you can drape a large piece of cheesecloth over a wide-mouth jar or deep but narrow bowl and secure the cheesecloth with a rubber band. Then pour the yogurt onto the cheesecloth.

The labneh is ready when it is very thick but not as thick as cream cheese. Transfer this to a bowl or container and stir in the salt. You can now mix in any add-ins, or simply sprinkle them on top when ready to serve. Drizzling with olive oil takes it over the top! Store in the refrigerator for about 2 weeks, or in the freezer for longer.

Yogurt

It was an Egyptian cook who first took the mystery out of yogurt for me. I was in Cairo during a gap year in college, staying with the parents of some college friends whose father was the *Los Angeles Times* correspondent in the Middle East. The whole month in Egypt left an indelible cultural and historical imprint in my mind, but I must admit that one of my most vivid memories was learning how to make yogurt: warm milk combined with a little leftover yogurt from the last batch, then put in a clean jar, wrapped with a few towels, and left to sit on the counter all day to be transformed into a thick, tangy delight. In this day of technological gadgets in the kitchen, we sometimes forget how we don't need special equipment to make magic, as cooks once did.

Why the towels? Towels maintain a warm temperature to allow the heat-loving lactic bacteria to thrive and grow, eating the milk sugar and acidifying and thickening it. As soon as I became vegan in my midtwenties, I applied the same technique to soy milk and found that it worked. Today, the yogurt that sits on store shelves is nothing like what I had in Egypt or even what was sold back in the '70s. It's milder, not as tangy, and full of sugar, gums, and fillers, having been adapted to modern taste buds. If you miss natural, tangy yogurt, the only recourse is to make your own—and it's so easy!

Plant milks, however, are all unique in their nutritional properties, and hence not only do they not all behave the same as each other, but they don't behave like animal milk, either. Most of them won't thicken without some help, which explains why commercial varieties are so full starches and gums. In my exploration of plant-milk yogurt, I tried to find ways to create a thick, creamy consistency from the plant milk itself without relying on any adjuncts. Hence, you will find my rich and delicious Coconut–Mung Bean Yogurt (page 90) or the Almond-Chickpea Yogurt (page 93), where the beans act as the thickening agent, and for soy yogurt, a truly rich and creamy version is achieved by combining it with cashews. Wherever I can, I have tried to rely on the natural thickening properties of the whole food without adding anything else.

Technical Tips

There are a few technical things to remember in making yogurt. Start with clean equipment, sanitizing with vinegar or boiling water to avoid contamination by unwanted bacteria. Second, find a warm place where your yogurt can maintain a warm temperature. As I learned in Egypt, you don't really need fancy equipment like a yogurt maker—you can just keep your yogurt warm by wrapping the jar in a puffy jacket or putting it in a warm, sunny window. As mentioned before, yogurt cultures like heat, so it needs to maintain a temperature between 95° and 110°F for 6 to 16 hours, depending on how tangy you like it.

For years, I had the belief that the optimal temperature for making yogurt was around 110°F, and that it never took longer than 8 hours. However, after much experimentation, I've found that kick-starting it at the usual 110°F and then dropping the temperature for a longer period results in thicker, creamier, tangier yogurts. As I think back to Cairo, this makes sense. A jar wrapped in towels would likely start out at a higher temperature but drop as it sits for hours. Lately, I've been starting at 110°F, and when the temperature drops down to 95°F after a couple of hours, I let it continue to ferment for around 12 hours to yield ultracreamy results.

YOGURT CULTURES

The cultures themselves can make a difference, some giving milder, others tangier, flavors. All yogurt cultures contain *L. bulgaricus* and *S. thermophilus*, but ones with *L. casei* increase the viscosity. Luckily, the recipes here utilize the thickening abilities of oats, cashews, and legumes to provide viscosity so that this is not as critical. However, many readers ask if they can use a probiotic capsule. Note that the bacteria differ with each brand, so make sure that the probiotics contain the cultures mentioned and not just acidophilus.

Finally, what about sweetening the yogurt or adding fruit? I highly recommend that this be done after the yogurt has set and chilled. Remember, it will all ferment, including the fruit, and too much sugar can be too much food for the bacteria, leading to gas development, lumpiness, and other undesirable traits.

HOW TO INCUBATE YOGURT

Don't overthink this—remember, yogurt has been made all over the world without any fancy equipment! Even today, I often make yogurt simply by heating the milk to the right temperature (around 110°F), pouring it into a sterilized mason jar, then wrapping the jar in a puffy jacket, blanket, or thick towel and leaving it on the counter. On a warm summer day, I might even just put the jar outside for a few hours, making sure it doesn't overheat. You just have to maintain a temperature above 90°F or as high as 110°F, keeping in mind that the lower the temperature, the longer it will take for it to become yogurt (that is, tangy and thick). If you are someone who prefers specialized equipment for any reason, there are several inexpensive options: A simple yogurt maker can be purchased online for less than $30, or you can use the yogurt setting on your Instant Pot. A proofing box or dehydrator also works, especially if you choose to use a lower temperature setting for a longer period.

SOY YOGURT TWO WAYS

While soy milk has been produced in Asia for millennia, soy yogurt was apparently invented in 1910 by a Chinese food scientist in Paris. For decades, before the more recent advent of almond, coconut, and other plant-based yogurts, soy yogurt was the only vegan type that could be found on store shelves.

Soy milk is one of the few plant milks that will thicken like animal milk when it interacts with lactic acid bacteria. Other plant milks need a little help from gums or starches to develop viscosity (except full-fat coconut yogurt, which is thick because of the fat content).

The gums, starches, and other thickeners added to most yogurts today—which were not added back in the 1970s—also help to stabilize the yogurt and prevent a little natural leakage of the whey, which, I guess, bothered some consumers. If you want a smooth, creamy yogurt instead of the old-fashioned kind that could leak a little whey, try making the Rich Soy-Cashew Yogurt.

Plain Soy Yogurt

MAKES 4 CUPS (950ML)

4 cups (950ml) Rich and Refreshing Soy Milk (page 58) or store-bought soy milk

¼ teaspoon nondairy yogurt starter, such as Vegurt, or about 3 tablespoons nondairy yogurt, homemade or store-bought

In a saucepan, heat the soy milk to about 110°F. Pour this into a sterilized 1-quart (1L) jar with a lid. Stir in the yogurt culture and keep at a warm temperature between 90° and 110°F for 8 to 16 hours, until it is as tangy as you like. It will further thicken when chilled. (See page 82 on how to incubate yogurt.) Store in the refrigerator for 2 to 3 weeks. Some whey at the top is normal.

CONTINUED

Rich Soy-Cashew Yogurt

MAKES 4½ CUPS (1.1L)

4 cups (950ml) Rich and
Refreshing Soy Milk (page 58)
or store-bought soy milk

Generous ¾ cup (112g)
cashews

¼ teaspoon vegan dairy
culture, such as Vegurt, or
2 to 3 tablespoons nondairy
yogurt, homemade or
store-bought

This version is creamier than the preceding.

IN A BLENDER, combine the soy milk and cashews and process until
rich and creamy. Pour the mixture into a medium saucepan.

Bring the mixture to a simmer over medium heat, stirring almost
constantly with a whisk or silicone scraper. The mixture should thicken
slightly. Pour into a sterilized container with a lid and let cool in the
refrigerator or freezer, stirring occasionally, until the temperature falls
below 110°F.

Stir in the yogurt culture and keep in a warm place at a temperature
between 90° and 110°F for 8 to 16 hours, until it is as tangy as you like.
It will further thicken when chilled. Store in the refrigerator for 2 to
3 weeks.

Soy Yogurt Cheese

MAKES 8 TO 12 OUNCES
(225G TO 340G)

This was one of my earliest experimentations with vegan cheese
decades ago. You simply need to pour 1 quart (1L) of yogurt into a nut
milk bag or over a large piece of cheesecloth, then attach to a faucet or
someplace so the whey can drain below into a sink or bowl, then drain
overnight or longer. As the whey drains off, the yogurt will thicken and
eventually result in something akin to a soft cheese. Stir in some salt,
some seasonings to taste (such as lemon zest, fresh herbs, or spices),
then refrigerate until it is firm enough to roll into a log or other shape,
or simply serve in a little dish.

THICK OAT-CASHEW YOGURT

MAKES ABOUT 5 CUPS (1.2L)

4 cups (950ml) water

1 cup (100g) rolled oats

¾ cup (100g) cashews

¼ teaspoon vegan yogurt culture, such as Vegurt, or 2 to 3 tablespoons nondairy yogurt, homemade or store-bought

While many commercial plant-based yogurts are thickened using gums and starches, this one gets its wonderfully thick and creamy texture from rolled oats, so it's super healthy as well. Oats contain something called beta glucan, a heart-healthy soluble fiber that also contributes to the incredibly thick texture of this yogurt. You can make it as sweet or tangy as you like by varying the time you culture it.

IN A BLENDER, combine the water and oats and process for about 1 minute to make oat milk. Pour the mixture through a nut milk bag and squeeze to extract as much milk as possible into a bowl. You will end up with just a little bit of oat pulp.

Return the milk to the blender and combine with the cashews and reprocess until smooth. Pour this milk into a 2-quart (2L) saucepan and heat, stirring, until it thickens like gravy (168° to 175°F).

Transfer this mixture to a sterilized jar or other container in which you will be culturing the yogurt, cover loosely, and refrigerate until it has cooled (after stirring) to 110°F or below.

Stir in the yogurt culture and keep in a warm place where it will hold a temperature between 90° and 110°F for 8 to 16 hours, until it is as tangy as you like. It will further thicken when chilled. Store in the refrigerator for 2 to 3 weeks.

PUMPKIN SEED–OAT YOGURT

MAKES A GENEROUS 4 CUPS (1L)

1 cup (160g) pumpkin seeds

¾ cup (76g) rolled oats

4 cups (950ml) water

¼ teaspoon vegan yogurt culture, such as Vegurt, or 2 to 3 tablespoons nondairy yogurt, homemade or store-bought

As with the Thick Oat-Cashew Yogurt (page 86), oats help to add a thick, creamy consistency to this, while the pumpkin seeds deliver protein.

IN A BLENDER, combine the pumpkin seeds, oats, and water and process for a minute or two until smooth and creamy. Pour the mixture into a nut milk bag and squeeze to extract as much milk as possible into a medium saucepan.

Set the saucepan over medium heat and heat until the mixture bubbles and thickens and reaches 160° to 170°F. Pour into a sterilized 1-quart (1L) glass jar and refrigerate until it has cooled down to 110°F or slightly below.

Stir in the yogurt culture and keep in a warm place at a temperature between 90° and 110°F for 8 to 16 hours, until it is as tangy as you like. It will further thicken when chilled. Store in the refrigerator for 2 to 3 weeks.

WATERMELON SEED KERNEL MILK YOGURT

MAKES A GENEROUS 4 CUPS (1L)

4 cups (950ml) Watermelon Seed Kernel Milk (page 54)

3 tablespoons cornstarch or arrowroot

1 teaspoon agar-agar powder

¼ teaspoon vegan yogurt culture, such as Vegurt, or 2 to 3 tablespoons nondairy yogurt, homemade or store-bought

Rich and creamy watermelon seed kernel milk makes great yogurt. Because watermelon seed kernel milk curdles and separates when heated, even at low temperatures, for an extended period, it needs to be thickened and stabilized with agar and a starch.

IN A MEDIUM saucepan, combine the milk, cornstarch, and agar and whisk well. Bring to a simmer over medium heat, frequently whisking and scraping the bottom with a silicone spatula. Let the mixture cook for a minute or two until it is like a thin sauce. Pour into a sterilized 1-quart (1L) glass jar and put it in the refrigerator or freezer to cool down to about 110°F, stirring occasionally.

Stir in the yogurt culture and keep at a warm temperature between 90° and 110°F for 8 to 16 hours, until it is as tangy as you like. It will further thicken when chilled. Store in the refrigerator for 2 to 3 weeks.

COCONUT–MUNG BEAN YOGURT

MAKES 4 CUPS (1L)

2 cups (470ml) water

One 13.5-ounce can full-fat coconut milk

1 cup (200g) moong dal (yellow split mung beans)

2 tablespoons maple syrup or organic sugar

¼ teaspoon vegan yogurt culture, such as Vegurt, or 2 to 3 tablespoons nondairy yogurt, homemade or store-bought

This has quickly grown to become my favorite yogurt—incredibly thick and creamy, it's almost like dessert, and yet it's high in protein. Coconut yogurts are generally rich because they are so high in fat without much other nutrition. Add mung beans, however, and you can feel good about getting some nutrition as well as flavor—in fact, you'll be getting about 12 grams of protein per 1-cup serving. This yogurt is best with a little sweetener to counteract any beany taste, although some may not be bothered by that at all.

IN A BLENDER, combine the water, coconut milk, and moong dal and process on high speed for a minute or so until smooth and creamy. Pour the mixture into a nut milk bag and squeeze to extract as much milk as possible into a medium saucepan.

Set the pan over medium heat and bring the milk to a simmer, whisking almost constantly, occasionally scraping the bottom and sides of the pot to ensure uniform heating and prevent the mung bean starch from settling and separating (without almost constant whisking, little shards of hard white gel can form). The mixture will become very thick as it cooks; it is ready when it looks like sour cream. Remove from the heat and pour into a sterilized 1-quart (1L) glass jar. Refrigerate to cool to 110°F.

Stir in the yogurt culture and keep at a warm temperature between 90° and 110°F for 8 to 16 hours, until it is as tangy as you like. It will further thicken when chilled. Store in the refrigerator for 2 to 3 weeks.

ALMOND-CHICKPEA YOGURT

MAKES A GENEROUS 4 CUPS (1L)

2 cups (300g) almonds

1 cup (200g) dried chickpeas

4 cups (950ml) water

¼ teaspoon vegan yogurt culture, such as Vegurt, or 2 to 3 tablespoons nondairy yogurt, homemade or store-bought

Unlike most almond milk yogurts that are thickened with starches and gums, this yogurt gets help from versatile chickpeas. Because it's fermented, however, the beans don't taste super beany and simply act to boost the viscosity and protein.

PUT THE ALMONDS and chickpeas in a large bowl and pour enough water over them so they can double in volume, 4 to 5 inches above the beans. Cover the bowl and let soak for 8 to 12 hours. Drain the water and rinse well.

In a blender, combine the almonds, chickpeas, and the 4 cups (950ml) water and process until creamy. Pour the mixture into a nut milk bag or cheesecloth and squeeze to extract the milk into a large pot. (Reserve the pulp for another use; see pages 183 to 199.)

Set the pot over medium heat and bring to a simmer, stirring often with a whisk, until thickened. Let this cool to 110°F or below; it will become thicker as it cools.

Stir in the yogurt culture and maintain a temperature between 90° and 110°F for 8 to 16 hours, until it is as tangy as you like. It will further thicken when chilled. Store in the refrigerator for 2 to 3 weeks.

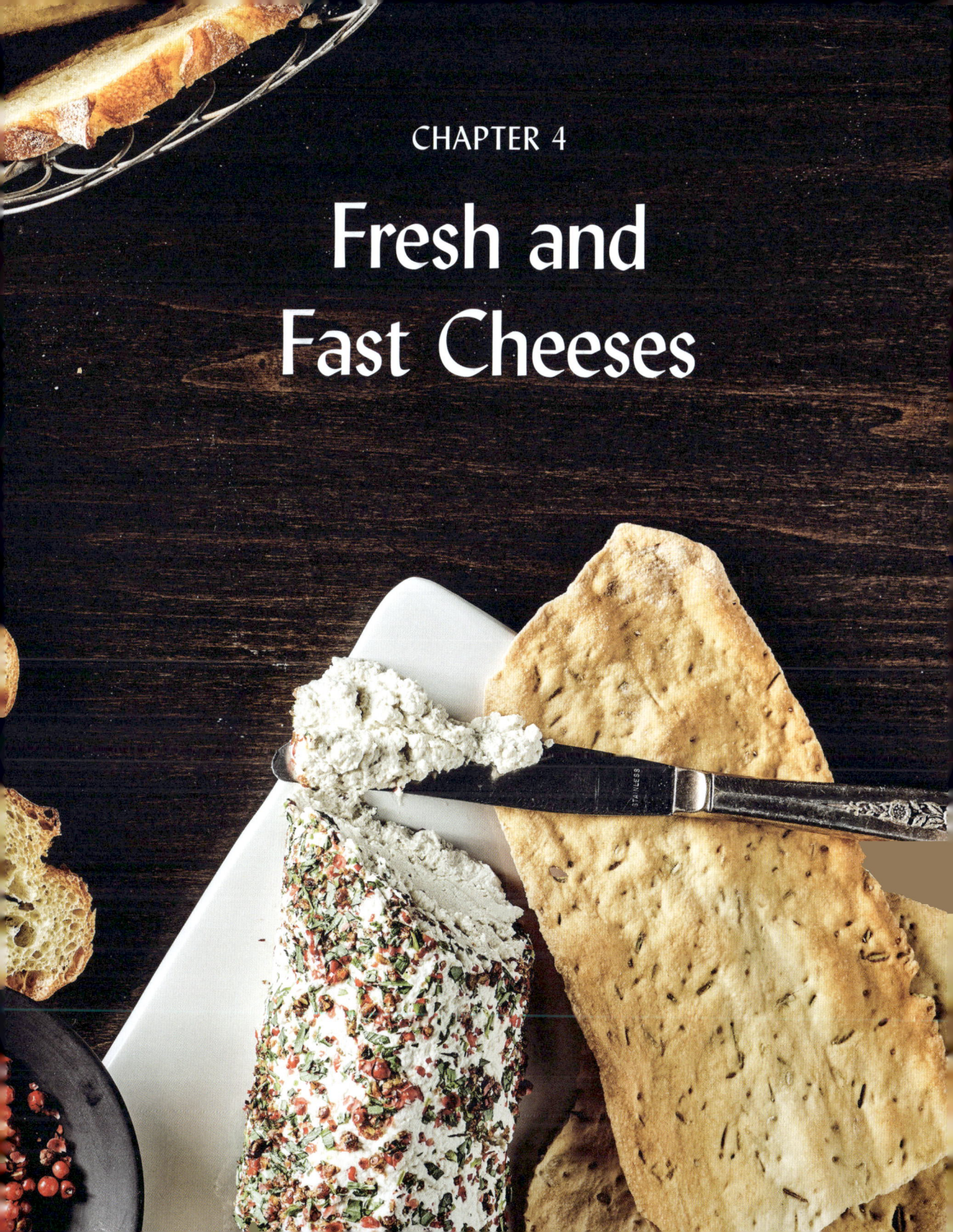

CHAPTER 4

Fresh and Fast Cheeses

This chapter is devoted to cheeses that are considered "fresh," meaning they do not undergo an aging or ripening process, although they are still cultured or fermented. This is a good place to start if you've never made cheese of any sort. Still, be aware that even fresh cheeses require a day or two to be ready!

Earlier renditions of my cheeses, while still fermented, started out more like pastes than coagulated milk curds. In this chapter, you'll see techniques that involve making curds and whey, more closely mimicking the process for traditional cheesemaking, but with differences because each plant milk is unique in its own properties. Most of the recipes involve fermentation, and you'll find in the next chapter that many also involve a long aging or ripening with molds. There is much to explore!

As covered in the beginning of this book, sanitation is needed for success in making cheese. We want to encourage the growth of certain organisms, from healthy lactic acid bacteria to perhaps *Penicillium candidum* (the fuzzy white mold on cheeses such as Brie), while discouraging the growth of unwanted ones. Starting with a clean milk as well as sterilized equipment and materials from start to finish is key. Don't skip steps such as sterilizing cheesecloth or pasteurizing nuts or milk as called for. At some point in the process of making any of these cheeses, there will be a pasteurization step, whether by boiling the nuts or seeds or heating the milk. You may still have luck bypassing this critical step, but it is essentially the luck of the draw, and next time, it may not turn out as well. In the world of bacteria, it can be the Wild, Wild West, so take a moment and sterilize your equipment. Generally speaking, immersing supplies in boiling water for a minute or two will do the job.

Despite my emphasis on sanitation, however, we should remember that historically cheese was made in less-than-sanitary conditions, which actually explains how certain cheeses were even "discovered" or "invented." It's said that Roquefort was created when a shepherd tucked away a chunk of cheese in the crevice of a rock when he went off to pursue a young lass, and when he returned days later to retrieve the cheese, found it covered in blue mold. Clearly, the young man wasn't thinking about sanitation! Cheeses were aged in actual caves, often becoming "contaminated" with a variety of molds, yeasts, and bacteria, many of which led to "discoveries" of new, now classic, cheeses such as Brie or Limburger. So you, too, could discover something new, but let's play it safe and try to control our environment as much as possible.

SUNNY CREAM CHEESE AND MASCARPONE

MAKES ABOUT 1¾ CUPS (375G)

2 cups (280g) sunflower seeds

3 cups (710ml) water

¼ cup (60ml) full-fat coconut milk or cream

2 tablespoons (30ml) distilled white vinegar

2 teaspoons calcium sulfate

¼ teaspoon fine sea salt

⅛ teaspoon vegan mesophilic culture

Thick, lovely, and as tangy (or not) as you like it, with protein to boot—this is truly a wonderful cream cheese for everything from morning bagels to a New York cheesecake. Unlike many of the commercial vegan cream cheeses made with just oil and starch, this has no added oils, so it won't melt into a pool of oil. At the beginning of the process, it will look very brown—but fear not—it will fade to a lovely white.

IN A BLENDER, combine the sunflower seeds, water, and coconut milk and process on high speed until smooth and creamy. Pour the mixture into a nut milk bag and strain into a saucepan. (Reserve the pulp for another use; see pages 183 to 199.) The milk will be thick and brown; don't be alarmed, the vinegar in the next step will whiten it.

Set the saucepan over medium heat and bring to a simmer. Add the vinegar, calcium sulfate, and salt and allow to curdle until you can see some whey separation and the cheese turn whiter. (It will turn even whiter after fermentation and draining.)

Turn off the heat and transfer to a sterilized 1-quart (1L) glass jar or container. Allow it to cool to below 90°F. Stir in the culture with a sterilized spoon and put in a warm place where it will maintain a temperature around 90°F for about 10 hours to reach a pH of between 4.5 and 5.0, or until it is as tangy as you like it. (The lower the pH, the tangier it will be.) It will have thickened quite a bit.

Drape a clean piece of cheesecloth over a 1-quart wide-mouth jar or container so that it hangs halfway down the inside of the jar and attach it with a rubber band. Pour the curds into the cheesecloth. Drain the cheese in the refrigerator for at least 24 hours. You'll notice that the drained liquid will be brown and the cheese will have become whiter. Once the cheese is very thick, transfer to a glass container and stir well, which will make it creamier. If a very smooth appearance is desired, process briefly in a food processor.

Store in the refrigerator for 3 weeks.

CONTINUED

SUNNY CREAM CHEESE AND MASCARPONE

CONTINUED

Mascarpone

MAKES 2 CUPS (450G)

To make this buttery Italian delight that's a little lighter and less tangy than the cream cheese, follow the recipe on the preceding page but reduce the water by ¼ cup (60ml), increase the coconut milk to 1 cup (240ml), and add 2 tablespoons lemon juice along with the vinegar and calcium sulfate. Culture to a pH of 5.0 to 5.5 (higher than cream cheese) and drain as directed.

(NOTE)

To "culture" is dairy terminology that means to ferment something. A "cultured" butter or cheese is something that has had lactic bacteria added to it to undergo fermentation and lower the pH.

A TALE OF TWO RICOTTAS

I offer two versions of ricotta here, in case allergies are an issue. They are both light, creamy, and fluffy, and can be used in a variety of dishes from lasagna to cheesecake and more. Ricotta is not fermented, so this is one of the quickest recipes to make.

Almond–Pumpkin Seed Ricotta

MAKES 12 TO 16 OUNCES (375G TO 450G)

1 cup (140g) almonds (if not using a high-powered blender, soak for 8 hours in cold water, then drain and rinse)

½ cup (70g) pumpkin seeds

3 cups (710ml) water

1½ tablespoons lemon juice or distilled white vinegar

½ teaspoon fine sea salt

This is a delicate ricotta perfect for both sweet and savory delights.

IN A BLENDER, combine the almonds, pumpkin seeds, and water and process on high speed until smooth and creamy. Pour the mixture into a nut milk bag and squeeze to extract as much milk as possible into a saucepan. (Reserve the pulp for another use; see pages 183 to 199.)

Set the saucepan over medium heat and heat the milk to about 200°F, stirring gently a few times; you will see some mild curdling. Add the lemon juice and salt, stir, and let it sit for about 2 hours undisturbed, until curdled further.

Line a sieve with cheesecloth and set over a bowl. Pour the mixture through the sieve and let it drain until it resembles ricotta, 1 to 2 hours. Use immediately or store in a covered container in the refrigerator for up to 2 weeks.

CONTINUED

Watermelon Seed–Cashew Ricotta

MAKES ABOUT 1½ POUNDS (675G)

1 cup (140g) watermelon seed kernels

½ cup (70g) cashews

4 cups (950ml) water

½ teaspoon fine sea salt

Watermelon seed milk is really, well, milky. And used as the base for ricotta, it creates an incredibly milky flavor and delicate texture with a hint of grassiness, reminiscent of its dairy counterpart. Note that the addition of cashews is an imperative, not an option.

IN A BLENDER, combine the watermelon seeds, cashews, and water and process until a smooth milk is achieved. Pour this through a nut milk bag and squeeze to strain the milk into a pot. There will be only a small amount of pulp.

Heat the milk over medium-low heat, occasionally scraping the bottom and sides with a silicone spatula. As it heats up, tiny curds will form and solidify, with the boiling bubbles formed from the "whey." When almost the whole mass has formed curds, stir in the salt and then pour it through a sieve or ricotta mold set over a bowl. Let the mixture drain for 30 minutes to 1 hour, or longer in the refrigerator until it is as firm as you like.

Transfer to a storage container and store in the refrigerator for up to 2 weeks.

Ricotta with Pistachios, Capers, and Honey

Here's a fun way to serve the entire block of ricotta as an appetizer or a charcuterie platter.

Unmold the ricotta on a plate. Sprinkle on top of it ½ cup chopped pistachios and ¼ cup drained capers. Drizzle with about 2 tablespoons of vegan honey. Serve with freshly sliced bread or crackers.

REGGIE GOAT *PLUS* RUFUS, THE AGED GOAT

MAKES ABOUT 12 OUNCES (340G)

1 cup (140g) almonds (if not using a high-powered blender, soak for 8 hours in cold water, then drain and rinse)

½ cup (70g) pumpkin seeds

½ cup (70g) hemp hearts

3 cups (710ml) water

½ to 1 teaspoon citric acid (depending on level of final acidity desired)

1 teaspoon fine sea salt

¼ teaspoon vegan culture, either mesophilic or thermophilic

Freshly minced parsley, tarragon, or other fresh or dried herbs, or grated lemon zest or crushed peppercorns (optional)

Rufus and Reggie were the two goats who inspired me to start my sanctuary, Rancho Compasión. I often refer to Reggie, a pure-white beauty, and Rufus, a studly black-and-white wonder, as my "boyfriend goats" because they are just too darn handsome. Gentle, kind, and smart, Reggie and Rufus literally saved my life by coming to my rescue when I was being attacked by another animal.

Reggie and Rufus were found wandering around a field in Merced, California, when they were mere kids. As Alpine goats, they are a breed known for their milk. Only one problem—they were male and therefore useless for milk production. Like male calves, male kids are considered dispensable. Luckily, they were rescued by Animal Place, another sanctuary, then came to live with me in Nicasio. I quickly fell in love with them, taking them on hikes with my dogs. This was how it all began!

So I dedicate these goat-style cheeses to them. Reggie Goat is a light, white, tangy spread, lovely on the No-Waste Crackers (page 189) or atop a pizza with caramelized onions for contrast. It's coagulated with citric acid, which helps gives it tang. The hemp seed milk adds a bit of grassiness as it ages over a couple of weeks, creating a complex cheese. And if you "age" Reggie Goat, you get the firmer, sliceable, still melt-in-your-mouth Rufus Goat.

IN A BLENDER, combine the almonds, pumpkin seeds, hemp hearts, and water and process on high speed for about 1 minute, until as creamy as possible. Pour the mixture into a nut milk bag and squeeze to extract as much milk as possible into a medium saucepan. (Reserve the pulp for another use; see pages 183 to 199.)

CONTINUED

REGGIE GOAT *PLUS* RUFUS, THE AGED GOAT

CONTINUED

Set the saucepan over medium-low heat and bring to a simmer, scraping the bottom and sides with a silicone spatula as curds form. When it starts to simmer around the edges or reaches 200°F, add the citric acid and stir gently, using more if you prefer a cheese with more tang. (It will be very tangy at first, but this will mellow over time, so play around with the amount of citric acid based on how tangy you like your finished product.) Turn off the heat and allow the mixture to sit for 1 hour or so until the temperature falls to around 86°F.

Stir in ½ teaspoon of the salt and the culture. Using a rubber band, attach a piece of cheesecloth over a wide-mouth jar or container so that it drapes into the container a bit. Pour the cheese into the cheesecloth and cover it with the hanging cheesecloth or a piece of plastic wrap, then put it in a warm place where it can continue to drain at an ambient temperature around 90 degrees for 12 to 16 hours, until it reaches a very low pH, around 3.8.

Put the cheese (still draining) in the refrigerator overnight or up to 24 hours, until it is firm enough to roll into a log using plastic wrap; it should feel springy to the touch. After shaping into a log, roll it in fresh or dried herbs or spices as desired. If, however, the cheese still feels wet, remove from the cheesecloth, form it into a log or wheel, sprinkle with a little salt, then wrap it in a few layers of paper towels and put in the refrigerator for a day or so, changing out the paper towels if they get wet. The cheese should now be firm and springy in texture. The acidity will mellow out over time.

To keep it soft, wrap it in cheese paper or plastic wrap. Store in the refrigerator for 2 to 3 weeks.

CONTINUED

Rufus, the Aged Goat

**MAKES 8 TO 10 OUNCES
(225G TO 285G)**

Reggie Goat (page 105)

2 tablespoons (10g) activated charcoal

3 tablespoons (45ml) water

2 teaspoons fine sea salt

This stunning cheese coated in a black "paint" of activated charcoal reveals an ivory interior when sliced. As it ages, the cheese will firm up and become sliceable. Instead of activated charcoal, you can opt to roll the fresh cheese in dried herbs (such as herbes de Provence) and let it age that way as well.

MAKE REGGIE GOAT, following the preceding recipe, and roll it into a log. In a small bowl, combine the activated charcoal with the water and salt to make a thin "paint." Using a pastry brush, carefully brush the cheese log with the "paint."

Set the log on a cheese mat set over a wire rack and place in a wine fridge or refrigerator until the coating is dry, 4 to 8 hours. When the coating is dry, wrap the cheese in parchment paper and let it age in your refrigerator for 3 to 6 weeks to develop flavor and firm up. If it starts getting too hard to slice, wrap in plastic wrap to preserve it longer.

(**NOTE**)

The cheese can also simply be coated directly in activated charcoal, although this method can be very messy. Put a tablespoon or so of activated charcoal on a sheet of parchment and simply roll the log around on it until it has been completely coated. Be careful, as the charcoal can get everywhere.

POTATO CASHEW MUENSTER

MAKES ABOUT 10 OUNCES (285G)

4 ounces (115g) peeled and large dice potatoes, any kind

1½ cups (360ml) water

½ cup (70g) cashews

2 tablespoons rolled oats

3 ounces (100g) deodorized shea butter or refined coconut oil, cut into pieces

3 tablespoons tapioca starch

3 tablespoons mochi rice flour

2 tablespoons nutritional yeast flakes

1½ teaspoons sea salt

¼ teaspoon vegan thermophilic culture

5 teaspoons agar-agar powder

1½ teaspoons psyllium husk powder

This is another quick and mild cheese for everyday sandwiches and snacking, deliciously gooey when melted but tasty cold as well.

IN A SMALL saucepan, combine the potatoes with water to cover. Bring to a boil and cook until fork-tender, 10 to 15 minutes. Drain well.

Transfer the drained potatoes to a blender and process until they get gooey. Add ½ cup (120ml) of the water, the cashews, and oats and process until smooth and creamy. The mixture will be warm.

Add the shea butter or coconut oil to the blender and process; the heat of the mixture should be enough to melt and incorporate it. Add the tapioca starch, mochi flour, nutritional yeast, and salt and process again.

Check the temperature of the mixture and, if hot, let it cool to 110°F or below; then add the culture and blend for a few seconds. Transfer to a sterilized container with a lid and place in a warm place to maintain that temperature for 16 hours or so to reach a pH of 4.7 to 5.0.

In a small saucepan, whisk together the remaining 1 cup (240ml) water and the agar. Cover and bring to a boil over medium-low heat and cook until it runs like molten glass off your whisk or spatula or reaches a temperature of 208°F.

Meanwhile, return the cheese mixture to a blender, add the psyllium powder, and blend briefly to combine. Prepare a cheese mold or other container by oiling it or lining with cheesecloth and have at the ready.

Pour the hot agar into the blender and process briefly to combine. Then pour this mixture back into the pot and cook until very thick, gooey, and stretchy. Pour this into the prepared cheese mold and refrigerate until solidified. It will have a Muenster-like, medium-firm, slightly flexible texture. Store wrapped in parchment paper in the refrigerator for 2 to 4 weeks, where it will get a little firmer over time.

PEPPER SHEEP'S SUNFLOWER MILK CHEESE

**MAKES 6 TO 8 OUNCES
(200G TO 225G)**

1½ cups (360ml) water

1 cup (140g) sunflower seeds

1 tablespoon white vinegar, plus more as needed

1 teaspoon calcium sulfate

⅛ teaspoon vegan mesophilic culture

2 ounces (56g) refined shea butter or refined coconut oil, melted

1 teaspoon fine sea salt

Pepper is a lovable male sheep with a freckled muzzle that looks as if he was sprinkled with black pepper. He and his brother, Salt, came to Rancho Compasión when they were just two days old as "bummer lambs." My daughter and I raised them in the house, bottle feeding them every 4 hours. Unfortunately, lambs are very delicate, and Salt did not make it past a month old, but Pepper has grown into a big, beautiful young male who still charms us even when he breaks into the house for treats like sunflower seeds.

Note that the vinegar in the recipe is not for adding acidity but to help whiten the cheese, which would be a grayish-tan because of the sunflower seeds. This cheese is milder and softer than Reggie Goat (page 105), but the shea butter adds firmness and an incredibly buttery mouthfeel.

IN A BLENDER, combine the water and sunflower seeds and process on high speed until smooth and creamy. Pour the mixture into a nut milk bag and squeeze to extract as much milk as possible into a saucepan. (Reserve the pulp for another use; see pages 183 to 199.) The milk will be thick and brown.

Set the saucepan over medium heat and bring to a simmer. Add the vinegar and calcium sulfate and allow it to curdle until you can see some whey separation and the cheese turn whiter; you can add up to an additional tablespoon of white vinegar to bleach even more, although it will turn even whiter after fermentation and draining.

Turn off the heat and transfer to a sterilized jar or glass container. Allow it to cool to below 90°F. Stir in the culture using a sterilized spoon and put in a warm place with a temperature around 90°F for about 16 hours, until a pH of between 4.5 and 5.0 is reached. It will have thickened quite a bit.

Using a rubber band, attach a piece of cheesecloth over a wide-mouth jar or container so that it drapes into the container a bit. Pour the cheese into this and let it drain for several hours at room temperature. You should end up with about 6 ounces (175g) sunflower milk cheese.

In a small food processor, combine the cheese, melted shea butter, and salt. Process until fully incorporated. Line your mold of choice with cheesecloth or plastic wrap (the mixture will be quite runny), pour in the cheese, and refrigerate for several hours until firm.

Store wrapped in plastic wrap in the refrigerator for 2 to 3 weeks. To age it and allow it to get firmer, wrap in cheesecloth or parchment. As it dries out, it will become sliceable and sharper in flavor.

Variations

LEMON PEPPERCORN
SUNFLOWER MILK CHEESE

Add 1 teaspoon grated lemon zest and 2 tablespoons coarsely ground black pepper to the food processor along with the shea butter.

HERB AND GARLIC
SUNFLOWER MILK CHEESE

Add 2 tablespoons fresh herbs of choice (tarragon, basil, chives, parsley, thyme, rosemary) along with 2 minced garlic cloves to the food processor along with the shea butter.

THE FOUNDATIONAL CASHEW CHEESE

MAKES 1 POUND (450G)

2 cups (280g) cashews

½ cup (120ml) water
or rejuvelac (see page 28)

1 teaspoon fine sea salt

2 tablespoons shio-kōji
(optional; for umami flavor)

1 tablespoon nutritional yeast
flakes

¼ teaspoon vegan culture,
either mesophilic or
thermophilic (omit if using
rejuvelac)

Cashew cheeses are now ubiquitous, and everyone makes them a little differently. Unlike the previous recipes in this chapter where a milk is coagulated, then separated from the whey, cashew cheese is basically a thick puree or paste that "sets up" into cheese. Sometimes coconut or another oil is added to make the mouthfeel even creamier, although I don't find it necessary.

Cashew cheese is the easiest of all to make and can be flavored in a multitude of ways. It can even be aged, and its texture will change over time from creamy to sliceable. I have aged wax-covered cashew cheese for even two years or longer, at which point the texture can become like Parmesan. Although in my first book I recommend air-drying, if you do this for too long without a protective coating, the flavor can dissipate and just become chalky. This is why a long-aged cashew cheese should be waxed or have another protective coating, such as herbs, a saturated oil like shea butter, or activated charcoal.

This recipe is a springboard from which I hope you will create your own versions.

IN A SAUCEPAN, combine the cashews with water to cover. Bring to a boil for 2 to 3 minutes, then drain well.

In a blender, combine the cashews, the ½ cup (120ml) water or rejuvelac, salt, shio-kōji (if using), and nutritional yeast and process until smooth and creamy, 1 to 2 minutes. Check the temperature—if the mixture is very hot, allow it to cool to below 100°F before adding the culture. Add the culture and reblend momentarily.

Transfer the mixture to a sterilized container with a lid, ensuring that there is at least an inch or two of headspace, and place in a warm place (80° to 90°F for mesophilic cultures, 90° to 105°F for thermophilic) for up to 24 hours. You should see little gas bubbles build up—this is a unique function of cashew fermentation (this does not happen with most other milks). You should check the pH or taste it after 12 hours. Aim for a pH of 4.6 for a cheesy but not too tangy cheese (the longer you ferment it, the tangier it will get).

When it has reached the desired pH, put the container in the refrigerator or transfer to a cheesecloth-lined mold of choice. Refrigerate it for 24 hours or so until it has firmed up and can be unmolded. Serve as is, or roll in fresh or dried herbs, smoked paprika, grated lemon zest, or crushed peppercorns. To keep and serve as a soft cheese, wrap in plastic wrap and store in the refrigerator for 2 to 4 weeks.

Variations

AGED CASHEW CHEESE

Cashew cheese is easier to age if it is coated in something that adds not only flavor but protection. Coat the molded cheese in dried herbs of choice, activated charcoal, or paprika and wrap loosely in parchment paper. Store in the refrigerator, where it will firm up and develop additional flavor over the course of 4 to 8 weeks. The cheese is ready when you say it is!

SAVORY AGED CASHEW CHEESE (CHEDDAR-LIKE)

When making the cheese, use only ⅓ cup (80ml) water or rejuvelac, increase the nutritional yeast to 4 tablespoons, and add 2 tablespoons light or white miso. Ferment until fairly tangy, aiming for a pH of 4.3 or lower. Put in a mold and refrigerate to firm up. Take out and wrap in parchment paper. Let it age in your refrigerator for 6 to 8 weeks, until firm and sliceable.

DOUBLE CREAM CHEESE

After fermentation, put the cheese in a food processor with ¼ cup (60ml) melted refined coconut oil or refined shea butter and process until smooth. At this point, you can also add finely minced chives, garlic, or fresh or dried herbs. Pour into a cheesecloth-lined mold of choice and refrigerate until firm, then remove from the cheesecloth. Wrap in plastic wrap or parchment paper and store in the refrigerator for up to 8 weeks.

FRESH WATERMELON SEED KERNEL MOZZARELLA

MAKES 1 POUND (450G)

1 cup (140g) watermelon seed kernels (see Resources, page 201)

2 cups (470ml) water

1 tablespoon agar-agar powder

⅓ cup (75g) unsweetened nondairy yogurt, such as Thick Oat-Cashew Yogurt (page 86), Watermelon Seed Kernel Milk Yogurt (page 89), Soy Yogurt (page 83), or Rich Soy-Cashew Yogurt (page 85), or a store-bought variety

6 tablespoons (80ml) neutral-tasting oil, such as avocado or grapeseed

¼ cup (40g) tapioca starch

1½ teaspoons fine sea salt

1¼ teaspoons psyllium husk powder

½ teaspoon lactic acid

Mozzarella is the most consumed cheese in America, and that's because of pizza, which a third of Americans consume at least once a week. Because mozzarella is high in protein, many deem pizza good, solid food for families. We know how animals are affected in the making of dairy mozzarella. And sadly, most commercial vegan mozzarellas are simply saturated fats congealed with starch, contributing no nutrition whatsoever. With this version, I've tried to create a creamy, pliable cheese that melts and browns beautifully but is also absolutely delightful cold, while also being nutritious. It is the "milkiest" mozzarella I've tasted, as if it were made from fresh cow's milk. And it's also one of the fastest cheeses in the book to make because it isn't fermented (it gets its cultured flavor from yogurt and lactic acid) and can therefore be ready in an hour to use for Caprese salad or melted on a pizza.

Most vegan mozzarellas have no substance when melted, turning into a sauce, sometimes sticky, sometimes just runny. Here, the structure of the watermelon seed kernel combined with psyllium husk leaves a bit of a chew even after it's been melted.

IN A BLENDER, process the watermelon seed kernels to a powder. Add the water and process to make a creamy milk, scraping the blender jar if needed to make sure no seeds are stuck on the bottom or sides. Pour the mixture into a nut milk bag and strain into a saucepan.

Set the saucepan over medium heat, scraping the bottom slowly and regularly to lift the curds; they should be large. Cook until the pan is mostly curds with some milky whey bubbling up, 8 to 10 minutes. Pour through a sieve set over a bowl. Let the whey cool for about 10 minutes until it is lukewarm.

Pour the whey back into the saucepan and whisk in the agar. Cover it and bring to a boil over medium heat.

Meanwhile, transfer the curds to a blender and add the yogurt, oil, tapioca starch, salt, psyllium powder, and lactic acid and process until

CONTINUED

Fresh Watermelon Seed Kernel Mozzarella Step-by-Step Process

smooth. Do not do this step until the agar is almost ready, for if it is allowed to sit for too long, the psyllium husk will thicken the mixture too much, making it difficult to work with.

When the agar has come to a boil and runs like molten glass off your whisk, pour it into the blender with the other ingredients and blend briefly to combine. Then pour it back into the pot and cook, whisking almost constantly, until very, very thick, gooey, and stretchy.

Now you have several choices for forming the cheese:

For a brick Simply pour it into any lightly oiled heatproof container.

For cheese balls Use an ice cream scoop to drop balls into ice water and allow to chill for 20 to 30 minutes until firm.

For a log Pour onto a sheet of parchment or cheesecloth, allow it to cool briefly, and then roll it into a log for easy slicing. (I do not recommend using plastic wrap with a hot cheese as it can leach endocrine disrupters.)

NOTE

If a firmer mozzarella is desired, increase the agar to 1½ tablespoons.

Refrigerate the cheese for several hours to firm up until sliceable. You can shred the cheese on the large holes of a box grater. It's best to put the cheese in the freezer for 20 minutes before doing so.

Fresh Baking Curds

This is a delicious and easy way to make cheesy curds for baking in dishes such as lasagna, a cheesy potato casserole, or even in a hot pasta dish in a skillet. Watermelon seed kernel milk coagulates when heated and creates soft, large curds that are wonderful.

AFTER MAKING THE watermelon seed kernel milk and passing it through the nut milk bag, put it back in the blender with everything else except the tapioca and agar, and simply blend. You can now use this "milk" in lasagna, casseroles, or a cheesy pasta bake. Simply pour on or over whatever you are making, then bake or apply heat in some way. It will form cheesy curds and exude minimal whey as it bakes or cooks.

MALLOUMI

MAKES 14 OUNCES (400G)

1½ cups (355ml) water

½ cup (100g) moong dal (yellow split mung beans)

¼ cup (55g) avocado or melted refined coconut oil

2 tablespoons nutritional yeast flakes

1½ teaspoons sea salt

¼ teaspoon vegan thermophilic culture

2 tablespoons tapioca starch

2 tablespoons potato starch

About 20 fresh mint leaves (optional)

I've been vegan for so long that admittedly there are some dairy cheeses I've never had, Halloumi being one of them. A cheese that hails from the island country of Cyprus, Halloumi holds its shape when heated and doesn't melt, making it similar to paneer but with a different flavor. I was curious what it was like, so I read up on its characteristics and attempted a plant-milk alternative. I doubt my golden-hued "Malloumi," made from mung beans, is an exact replica, but it hits the mark when it comes to a tasty, creamy option that can be grilled. Consider it Halloumi's vegan cousin. Once firm, you can then grill, sauté, or fry in a little oil as desired. Serve as is or with a tasty topping, such as a mixture of diced fresh tomato, cucumber, and red or spring onions, and drizzle with olive oil.

IN A BLENDER, combine the water, mung beans, oil, nutritional yeast, and salt and process on high speed until smooth and creamy. Add the culture and process again.

Put it in a warm place where it will maintain a temperature between 95° and 100°F for 16 to 24 hours to reach a pH of around 4.6, or until it tastes cheesy to your liking.

Pour the mixture into a nut milk bag, squeezing to extract as much milk as possible into a saucepan. (Reserve the pulp for another use; see pages 183 to 199.)

Oil a heatproof square or rectangular baking pan, a Pyrex storage dish, or silicone molds that will allow the mixture to fill about ½ inch deep (you can use two smaller rather than one large dish if you like). Whisk the tapioca and potato starches into the Malloumi mixture, then pour into the prepared pan(s). If you want the mint flavor to permeate the cheese, stick in the mint leaves. Put the container(s) in a steamer, and steam, covered, until the top feels firm and the internal temperature is above 170°F, 15 to 20 minutes. Remove and let cool completely before unmolding, cutting, and using. To store, refrigerate (perhaps in the dish you steamed it in) for up to 2 weeks.

FRENCH-STYLE SOFT TRUFFLE CHEESE

MAKES TWO 12-OUNCE (340G) WHEELS

2¼ cups (535ml) water

⅔ cup (100g) almonds (if not using a high-powered blender, soak for 8 hours in cold water, then drain and rinse)

¼ cup (40g) pumpkin seeds

2 tablespoons hemp hearts

1 teaspoon nutritional yeast flakes

Fine sea salt

1 teaspoon calcium sulfate dissolved in 1 tablespoon water

¼ teaspoon vegan mesophilic culture

6 ounces (170g) mushrooms

1 tablespoon olive oil

1 teaspoon good-quality black truffle oil, or more to taste

½ cup (110g) refined coconut oil or refined shea butter, melted

2 tablespoons tapioca starch

1½ teaspoons agar-agar powder

This is simply delightful on a cheese board—wonderfully velvety in texture with complex umami flavors from the mushrooms, beckoning all guests. It comes together in 24 hours, so it's relatively easy to make as well. If you want to elevate this even further, you can grow *Penicillium candidum,* the white mold for Brie and Camembert, on it (see the recipe for Truffle Brie that follows). You can also use it to make a wonderfully elegant "mac and cheese," or use it in panini.

IN A BLENDER, combine 1¾ cups (415ml) of the water, the almonds, pumpkin seeds, and hemp hearts and process on high speed until smooth and creamy. Pour the mixture into a nut milk bag and squeeze to extract as much milk as possible into a medium saucepan. (Reserve the pulp for another use; see pages 183 to 199.)

To the milk in the saucepan, add the nutritional yeast and ½ teaspoon salt. Set over medium heat and bring to a simmer, frequently stirring and scraping the sides and bottom with a silicone spatula. Stir in the dissolved calcium sulfate and mix well. Pour this into a sterilized container and let it cool to 90°F.

Stir in the culture using a sterilized spoon, cover, and put in a warm place where it will maintain a temperature of around 90°F for 14 to 20 hours, until it has become mildly tangy with a pH between 4.5 and 4.9. Don't let it get too tangy, but remember, you must be the judge.

The next day, after the cheese has sufficiently cultured, start on the mushrooms. Quarter them and put in a food processor. Pulse until they are finely minced, but don't overprocess.

In a skillet, heat the olive oil over high heat. Add the mushrooms and a good pinch of salt and sauté until browned, about 2 minutes. They should not be watery or completely dry but look moist without sitting in a pool of water. Mix in the truffle oil. Set aside while you finish preparing the cheese.

Line two 6-inch (15cm) round silicone baking or cheese molds with a layer of at least 90-gauge cheesecloth with the cloth hanging over the sides. Pour the cheese into a blender and add the coconut oil and tapioca starch, processing for 30 seconds, until emulsified.

Meanwhile, in a small pot, whisk together the remaining ½ cup (120ml) water and the agar. Cover with a lid and bring to a boil over medium-low heat. When the agar is fully dissolved and runs clear like molten glass off the whisk, pour it quickly into the blender with the cheese and process briefly. Pour it back into the pot and cook, stirring frequently, until it is thick, goopy, and glossy.

Using a silicone spatula, swirl the mushrooms into the cheese so that a ribbon of mushrooms runs through the cheese; don't overmix. Pour the cheese into the cheesecloth-lined molds, smoothing the tops. Refrigerate overnight, until set and firm enough to unmold, then remove the cheesecloth. Store wrapped in wax paper in the refrigerator for 2 to 3 weeks.

Truffle Brie

Yes, you can grow *Penicillium candidum,* the fluffy white mold, on your truffle cheese, although it takes a little care. I also find that it works best in warmer weather when the mold grows quickly, rather than in winter. You will need to dry the cheese before spraying with the mold. After unmolding and removing the cheesecloth, sprinkle ½ teaspoon salt over the entire surface of the cheese. Set it on a wire rack, a clean cheese mat, or Japanese sushi mat (set on a cooling rack) and place in the refrigerator or in a cool place for 24 hours. Flip over and let sit another 12 to 24 hours, until the surface feels relatively dry.

Spray both sides of the cheese with *Penicillium candidum* Mold Spray (page 152). Place on a cheese mat on several layers of paper towels in a ripening box. Keep at around 60°F for 2 days, flipping and lightly spraying each day, until you begin to see mold growth. Then place into a wine fridge or refrigerator for another 10 to 14 days, until it is mostly covered in white mold. Store wrapped in cheese paper in the refrigerator for up to 30 days.

PANEER

MAKES 11 TO 12 OUNCES
(310G TO 340G)

2 cups (450ml) unsweetened
soy milk, homemade
(page 58) or store-bought
(make sure it has no sugar or
flavors, such as vanilla)

1 cup (140g) watermelon
seed kernels (see Resources,
page 201)

½ teaspoon sea salt

½ cup (120ml) water

4 teaspoons distilled white
vinegar

1 teaspoon agar-agar powder

The usual vegan "go-to" for paneer has been tofu, which looks
like paneer but lacks the creamier texture. This version contains a
mixture of soy milk and watermelon seed kernel milk to produce a
texture closer to its animal dairy cousin. Interestingly, the method
for making them is very similar as well. It can be fried, sautéed, or
added to curries.

IN A BLENDER, combine the soy milk, watermelon seed kernels, and salt
and blend on high speed until very smooth, 1 to 2 minutes. Pour the
mixture into a nut milk bag or cheesecloth, squeezing to extract as
much milk as possible into a saucepan. (Reserve the pulp for another
use; see pages 183 to 199.)

Set the saucepan over medium heat and heat until tiny foam starts
to form around the edges. While heating, scrape the curds from the
sides and bottom of the pan with a silicone spatula. Cook until about
25 percent of the milk has formed curds, then quickly proceed to the
next step.

In a small bowl, combine the water, vinegar, and agar. Stir this mixture
into the pan of milk. More curds will form. Cook for several minutes until
some clear whey starts to bubble up. Turn off the heat immediately—
the longer you cook the curds, the harder they will be, resulting in a
paneer that is grainy.

Line a sieve with a large piece of cheesecloth and set over a bowl. Pour
the curd mixture into the sieve, then gather up the loose ends of the
cheesecloth and tie them with a rubber band so that the cheese forms
a ball. Tie the cheesecloth around a faucet over a sink, or in some
other manner over a bowl, and let the cheese drain and cool until it is
firm and relatively dry, at least 3 to 4 hours. Do not press the cheese,
as it could crumble.

Unwrap the cheese. It is now ready to use. Cut into cubes to use
in curries and other dishes. Paneer keeps in the refrigerator for up
to 10 days.

KOHANA'S FAVORITE CHEESE FOR GRILLED CHEESE SANDWICHES

MAKES ABOUT 2 POUNDS (900G)

8 ounces (225g) cubed, peeled potatoes, any kind

6 ounces (170g) cubed, peeled orange sweet potatoes (Jewel or Garnet)

1 cup (140g) sunflower seeds

2¼ cups (540ml) water

1½ tablespoons distilled white vinegar

½ cup (112g) avocado oil

6 tablespoons nutritional yeast flakes

¼ cup (80g) white miso

2 teaspoons sea salt

¼ teaspoon vegan thermophilic culture

¼ cup (40g) tapioca starch

4 teaspoons psyllium husk powder

3 tablespoons agar-agar powder

This is a mild-flavored cheese designed for perfect gooey, stretchy grilled cheese sandwiches. My teenage niece, Kohana, was the first to put her stamp of approval on it and told me she almost cried when she ran out of the stash I had given her to take home. Allergen-free and made of healthy ingredients, such as potatoes and sunflower seeds, it's a kid-friendly cheese for all ages. If you're trying to avoid oil, you can omit it and it's still almost as good.

The potato provides a naturally gooey base, while the sweet potato lends color and a hint of sweetness, and the sunflower seeds provide both protein and fiber. You can also melt this down with some plant milk for mac and cheese.

PUT THE POTATOES and sweet potatoes in a pot large enough to hold them and cover with water. Bring to a simmer over medium heat. Cover and cook until fork-tender, 15 to 20 minutes. Drain well.

Meanwhile, bring a small pot of water to a boil. Add the sunflower seeds and boil for 1 to 2 minutes, then drain well in a sieve. Put the sunflower seeds into a sterilized blender jar, add 1 cup (240ml) of the water, and process until smooth and creamy. Add the vinegar and process; the mixture will become whiter. Add the avocado oil, nutritional yeast, miso, and salt and process again until creamy.

Add the potatoes to the sunflower mixture and process again until very creamy. The mixture will be very warm and need to be cooled down before culturing. Transfer the mixture to a sterilized container with a lid and put it in the refrigerator to cool down quickly.

CONTINUED

When the temperature has fallen to below 110°F, add the culture and put it in a warm place where it can maintain a temperature of around 100°F for 8 to 12 hours to reach a pH of between 4.4 and 4.8. The lower the pH, the sharper the cheese; the higher the pH, the milder the cheese (this cheese ferments very quickly).

Put the cheese back in a blender. Add the tapioca starch and psyllium husk and blend until combined. Oil a cheese mold of choice and have at the ready.

Meanwhile, in a pot, whisk the agar into the remaining 1¼ cups (300ml) water. Set the pot over medium heat, cover, and bring it to a boil. Cook until the agar is completely dissolved. Pour this into the other ingredients in the blender and process briefly. Then pour this back into the pot and cook over medium heat, alternately scraping with a silicone spatula and whisking, until it is very thick, stretchy, and glossy. Pour the cheese into the oiled mold and refrigerate for several hours or overnight, until it is firm enough to slice. It is a relatively soft cheese but should be sliceable—its purpose is for melting in sandwiches, so the fact that it isn't ultra-firm should not be problematic. Store in the refrigerator for 2 to 4 weeks.

> **NOTE**
>
> *For a firmer cheese, substitute 2½ tablespoons kappa carrageenan for the agar powder. After fermenting, pour the cheese back into a blender along with 1 teaspoon calcium sulfate, the tapioca starch, and psyllium husk powder, then add to the carrageenan mixture and cook until gooey and stretchy.*

MAGIC MOZZARELLA

MAKES 3½ CUPS (ABOUT 900ML)

3 cups (710ml) Watermelon Seed Kernel Milk (page 54), Cashew Milk (page 49), Lucky Pumpkin Seed Milk (page 50), Fortified Oat Milk (page 45), or Rich and Refreshing Soy Milk (page 58)

½ cup (112g) avocado, olive, or refined and melted coconut oil

5 tablespoons (50g) tapioca starch

2 teaspoons fine sea salt

¼ teaspoon vegan thermophilic culture

1 tablespoon psyllium husk powder

This mozzarella is in the form of a sauce that will magically solidify when exposed to heat. You can pour it on pizza or lasagna, or use it as a base for a mac and cheese (see Mac and Cheese Sauce, below).

IN A BLENDER, combine the milk, oil, tapioca starch, salt, and culture and puree until smooth and creamy. Pour this into a sterilized jar, cover with a lid, and set it in a warm place at 100°F for 8 to 12 hours, until it reaches a pH just below 5.0. At this point, you can proceed to the next step if you are going to use it immediately, or you can refrigerate for up to 2 weeks until you are ready to use it.

When you are ready to use it, return the mixture to a blender and add the psyllium husk powder and reblend (see Note). It is best to add the psyllium husk right before you plan to use it, as the longer it sits in the mixture, the thicker and goopier it will get, making it difficult to pour out or squirt out of a squirt bottle. In this case, you can still spoon it onto whatever you are baking.

NOTE

If you don't plan to use all the cheese right away, you can measure out 1 teaspoon of psyllium husk to each cup of cheese mixture you are using and add just that.

Variation

MAC AND CHEESE SAUCE

To turn this into a mild cheddar-flavored sauce for a quick mac and cheese, add ½ cup nutritional yeast flakes and 2 tablespoons white miso to the milk before you ferment it. Afterward, blend in (along with the psyllium) 2 teaspoons mustard powder and 1 teaspoon each of onion powder and paprika. You can heat this on the stovetop and it will thicken into a lovely sauce for macaroni.

"WHEY TO GO" SLICING CHEESE

MAKES ABOUT 1 POUND (450G)

1½ cups (375ml) whey from Rancho Rockfort (page 156), Nicasio Blues (page 160), High Sierra (page 145), Sunny Cream Cheese (page 99), Reggie Goat (page 105), or any curd cheese that requires draining

2 tablespoons potato starch

2 tablespoons tapioca starch

2 tablespoons nutritional yeast flakes

4 tablespoons (55g) avocado oil, olive oil, or melted refined coconut oil (or 6 tablespoons [84g] if using whey from a cheese that does not contain any oil, such as Reggie Goat)

2 tablespoons kappa carrageenan

1 teaspoon fine sea salt

The dairy industry churns out millions of pounds of processed cheese from the whey drained from the curds. So I was inspired to make my own whey-based cheese. Admittedly, it resembles the packaged slices and shreds you see at supermarkets—mild and decent enough for sandwiches and kids' snacks, but nothing you'd put on a cheese board. Still, it's quick and easy to make, and assures that nothing goes to waste. The whey from cheeses that contain oil work best, such as Rancho Rockfort, Nicasio Blues, or High Sierra Alpine-Style Cheese. You can also use whey from Sunny Cream Cheese, Reggie Goat, or any other fermented variety, but you'll have to add the larger amount of oil. While the cheese is not fermented, the whey itself is, and hence, a cheesy flavor will result.

OIL A MOLD (a small bread pan is a good choice for this one) and have at the ready.

In a medium saucepan, whisk together all the ingredients. Set over medium heat and cook, whisking almost constantly, until very thick and stretchy, 3 to 5 minutes. Pour into the oiled mold and put in the refrigerator to cool and harden. After several hours, you should be able to unmold and slice it. Keep Whey to Go cheese wrapped in parchment paper or a plastic bag in the refrigerator for 2 to 4 weeks.

Variation

SOFT "WHEY TO GO" CHEESE

This makes a slightly softer cheese but works well if you don't have kappa carrageenan. Measure out ½ cup (120ml) of the whey and set aside. In a saucepan, whisk together the remaining 1 cup (240ml) whey with the oil, nutritional yeast, and 3 tablespoons agar-agar powder, and bring to a fast simmer over medium heat. Dissolve the potato and tapioca starches in the reserved ½ cup whey and pour into the simmering pan. Cook until thick and stretchy, then pour into an oiled mold of choice. Store wrapped in parchment in the refrigerator for 2 to 3 weeks.

OVERNIGHT IN PARMA

**MAKES ABOUT 1 POUND
9 OUNCES (720G)**

½ cup (120ml) green olive
brine

¼ cup (60ml) water

¼ cup (60ml) sauerkraut juice

1¾ cups (245g) cashews
(or sunflower seeds if allergic)

⅔ cup (80g) chickpea flour

⅔ cup (150g) deodorized
cocoa butter, refined coconut
oil, or a combination, melted

½ cup (25g) nutritional
yeast flakes

3 tablespoons (90g) white
miso

¼ teaspoon vegan
thermophilic culture

Scant 1 cup (150g) potato
starch

2 teaspoons fine sea salt

Parmigiano-Reggiano may take 24 to 36 months to age in Parma, but in your house, this one will be ready overnight. Full of umami and flavor, whether shaved or grated over pasta, or used as the base for a great Cacio e Pepe (page 193), this cheese will become a family favorite.

IN A BLENDER, combine the olive brine, water, sauerkraut juice, and cashews and process on high speed until creamy and smooth. Add the chickpea flour, melted cocoa butter, nutritional yeast, and miso and process again until well incorporated. Add the culture and process briefly.

Transfer the mixture to a sterilized container and put in a warm place to maintain a temperature of 100° to 110°F for up to 24 hours to reach a pH of around 5.1.

Set up a steamer that can hold two 6-inch (15cm) round silicone or any Pyrex baking or storage pans or dishes that will allow the cheese to be 1 to 1½ inches in depth. I use a bamboo steamer, but you can set up a steamer using any pan with a rack, some water at the bottom, and a lid for the pan.

Stir the potato starch and salt into the cheese mixture and whisk well. Pour into the baking pans. Place into the steamer, cover, and steam until the top feels dry and the internal temperature has reached over 160°F, 15 to 20 minutes.

Refrigerate the cheese overnight until it is completely hard. Use wherever Parmesan is called for. Store in a covered container or plastic bag in the refrigerator for 2 to 3 months.

CHAPTER 5

Aged and Mold-Ripened Cheeses

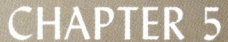

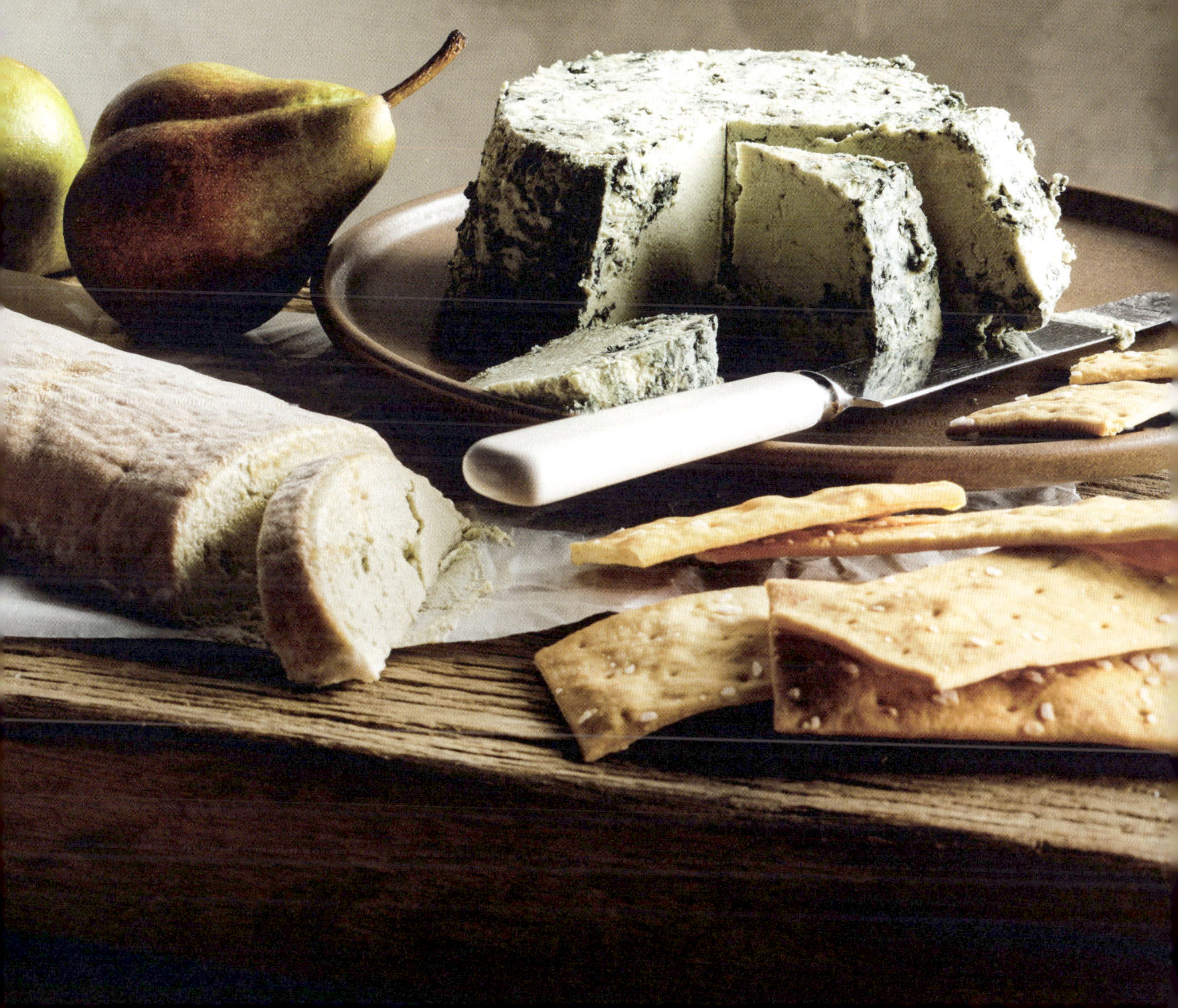

Waiting for a cheese to age or ripen can fill you with the kind of excitement a child feels waiting for a birthday. And sometimes, this requires patience. Whether it's Angel's Sharp Potato Cheddar (page 134), another aged cheese, or a mold-ripened blue such as Rancho Rockfort (page 156), a delicious blue inoculated with the mold *Penicillium roqueforti,* many of these will not reach their optimal state in terms of flavor or texture for weeks or months. And your cheese cave? It'll be either a wine fridge or your refrigerator, and you'll have the fun anticipation of checking in on them almost daily.

Just like animal dairy cheeses, these wonders require time for the bacteria, yeasts, and molds to do their thing, breaking down the proteins and fats, while achieving the desired textures and flavors. These are among the most challenging to make, so if you're new to cheesemaking, you may want to try one of the cheeses in the previous chapter first. One of the fresh cheeses, Reggie Goat (page 105), can be aged to become Rufus the Aged Goat. This could be a good place to start.

ANGEL'S SHARP POTATO CHEDDAR

**MAKES 1½ TO 2 POUNDS
(680G TO 910G)**

12 ounces (340g) waxy
potatoes, unpeeled and whole

2½ cups (600ml) water

Scant 1½ cups (200g)
pumpkin seeds

3½ ounces (100g) deodorized
cocoa butter, cut up

1¾ ounces (50g) refined or
deodorized coconut oil or
shea butter, cut up

2 tablespoons (60g)
white miso

1 cup (50g) nutritional
yeast flakes

1 teaspoon fine sea salt

¼ to ½ teaspoon liquid
annatto (optional; for color),
to taste

4 teaspoons agar-agar
powder

¼ teaspoon vegan
mesophilic culture

Angel is a rescued Guernsey dairy cow about the color of this cheese—a slightly orangish brown. She also has very sharp, big horns, and she knows it. Animals always know among themselves who has the biggest, baddest horns, and because of this, Angel is the diva of Rancho Compasión, lording over every other creature, including her devotee, Louie, a Black Angus heifer who idolizes her. Luckily, her milk isn't needed to make this full-flavored cheddar because we've turned to potatoes and pumpkin seed milk instead. This cheese is also cultured *after* forming in its mold, rather than before.

When I first embark on aged cheese experiments, I don't know for weeks or months how they will turn out. I moderate my expectations and try to approach the moment of truth with a bit of trepidation. So I was surprised and delighted when I cut into a waxed wheel of cheese I had made 8 or 9 months earlier and forgotten about. Although I wasn't expecting much, the cheese was beautifully firm and sliceable, filling my mouth with such umami and depth of flavor. For dinner, I couldn't stop eating slice after slice with homemade bread and a bowl of soup. I've been making this cheese ever since.

If you've gotten used to the store-bought vegan "Cheddar-style" slices (made of coagulated saturated fats, starch, and natural flavorings) available in supermarkets today, you'll likely be surprised as well with the richness and complexity of flavor of this cheese. Because it's aged, it won't be gooey and stretchy when melted, but it does soften and create a fantastic grilled cheese sandwich as well.

Since I have to wait a few weeks before I can enjoy this (as with other aged cheeses), I like to make a large wheel so there's plenty to last once it's finally ready! And if you really want to impress your guests, take it to the next level by turning it into the Drunken Cow (page 138).

IN A STEAMER basket, steam the potatoes until fork-tender, 30 to 40 minutes.

Meanwhile, in a blender, combine the water and pumpkin seeds and process until smooth and creamy, 1 to 2 minutes; you do not have to strain this milk.

Pour into a medium saucepan and cook over medium-low heat, scraping the bottom every 30 seconds or so, until the milk has fully curdled. There will be some slightly cloudy whey bubbling up between the curds.

Drain the curds through cheesecloth or a fine sieve set over a bowl and press gently. You should get about 1 cup (240ml) whey. Transfer the whey to a small pot and set aside. Put the hot curds into a bowl and stir in the cocoa butter and coconut oil until fully melted. Stir in the miso, nutritional yeast, and salt and set aside until the potatoes are ready.

When the potatoes are tender, remove from the steamer basket and submerge in cold water. Quickly peel the skins off, then put the peeled potatoes in a food processor. Process for a minute or two until gluey and stretchy. Add the curd mixture and process until smooth (if you are having trouble getting it to be smooth, you can transfer this to the blender again and process). Add the annatto (if using), adjusting the amount as desired, and process until a uniform color is achieved (without the annatto, your cheese will be more brown than orange). Leave the mixture in the food processor or blender and allow it to cool to around 80°F, give or take 10°F.

Prepare a sterilized round cheese mold or container large enough to hold the entire mixture, or you can divide it between two or more molds of choice. Line these with sterilized cheesecloth (see page 21) large enough to hang over the sides (you'll be covering the cheese with the cheesecloth).

CONTINUED

ANGEL'S SHARP POTATO CHEDDAR

CONTINUED

To the reserved whey in the small pot, add the agar and whisk to dissolve. Cover and cook until it boils and runs like molten glass off the whisk. Pour the agar mixture into the cheese and process until the agar has been incorporated, about 30 seconds. Finally, add the culture and process briefly.

Pour the cheese mixture into the prepared mold(s), smoothing the top with a rubber spatula, and drape the cheesecloth over the top. Put the cheese in a warm place where it can maintain a temperature of 85° to 90°F for 16 to 24 hours, until a pH of below 4.6 has been reached (the lower the pH, the sharper the cheese). Refrigerate the cheese overnight to firm up.

The next day, remove the cheese from the mold and carefully peel off the cheesecloth. You will now age the cheese in your refrigerator or wine fridge.

To age in the refrigerator: Wrap the cheese in parchment paper and place in the refrigerator for 4 weeks or longer, checking the cheese every couple of days and changing the parchment paper when it gets moist. If mold develops, scrape it off with a knife or paper towel dipped in vinegar, and rewrap in new parchment. After several weeks, the cheese will become firm and sliceable as it loses moisture and weight. The longer it ages, the firmer and more flavorful it gets. To age it further (up to 2 years), coat in wax (see How to Wax Cheese, page 38).

To age in a wine fridge: Brush melted refined cocoa butter on the cheese and place it on a cheese drying or cooling rack. Flip the cheese every few days and check for mold. If the solidified butter chips off, brush on another layer. Let it age for at least 6 to 8 weeks. To eat, chip or cut off the cocoa butter. To age it longer, coat in wax (see How to Wax Cheese, page 38).

The cheese can keep for months depending on how it is stored. If left in parchment after fully aging to a firm, sliceable consistency, it will become very dry over time, so it's best to transfer to a plastic bag or coat in wax after it has reached the desired consistency and hardness.

CONTINUED

Drunken Cow

This is undoubtedly one of the most popular cheeses when I serve it at parties. It is essentially the Angel's Sharp Potato Cheddar (page 134) soaked in a red wine brine for about 48 hours, then dried, creating a cheese with a complex, slightly tangy crimson exterior giving way to full-flavored, creamy richness. (Brining in wine is something I do with many cheeses, but I particularly like it for this cheese.) You'll need to make the Angel's cheddar first and let it age for at least 2 weeks until fairly firm before you brine it.

TO MAKE THE brine, pour 1 (750ml) bottle of red wine (it doesn't have to be expensive but should be drinkable) into a saucepan and stir in ¼ cup (60g) sea salt. Bring to a simmer, stirring until the salt dissolves completely. Pour the mixture into a container large and deep enough to cover the wheel of cheese and allow the brine to cool completely.

Then add the 2-week-aged cheese—it can be older as well, but it needs to be firm enough to hold together in the brine. Cover and let it bathe for a day, then flip over and brine for another day. Depending on how long the cheese has aged beforehand, it may be a little soft coming out of the brine—so exercise care.

Remove the cheese from the brine, let it drain on a cooling rack until dry, then wrap again in parchment and allow it to age for an additional 4 to 5 weeks.

DOG-GONE GOODA

MAKES 12 TO 14 OUNCES (350G TO 400G)

4 cups (950ml) water

1 cup (140g) watermelon seed kernels (see Resources, page 201)

½ cup (70g) hemp hearts

½ cup (70g) pumpkin seeds

½ cup (110g) unrefined shea butter, melted

1 cup (50g) nutritional yeast flakes

3 tablespoons (90g) white miso

1 teaspoon calcium sulfate

¼ teaspoon vegan thermophilic culture

2 teaspoons fine sea salt

My senior cattle-dog mix, Koan, limping from an ACL tear, somehow still managed to jump up onto the counter to steal and devour an entire block of this cheese. His look of satisfaction afterward said that it was doggone good.

This was one of the first cheeses I made without the addition of binders to hold the curds together. Just as in traditional dairy cheesemaking, I experimented with simply packing the curds together to see what would happen, and lo and behold—over time, they melted together into one smooth, creamy texture. I wasn't trying to make Gouda—I was simply experimenting with this technique, but a friend said it reminded her of a slightly smoky Gouda. With Koan's blessing, I decided to name it Dog-Gone Gooda—and yes, it was gone in an instant!

IN A BLENDER, combine the water, watermelon seed kernels, hemp hearts, pumpkin seeds, melted shea butter, nutritional yeast, and miso and process on high for a minute until smooth and creamy. Pour the mixture into a nut milk bag, squeezing to extract as much milk as possible into a medium saucepan. (Reserve the pulp for another use; see pages 183 to 199.)

Set the saucepan over medium heat and heat, using a silicone scraper to scrape the sides and bottom occasionally as curds begin to form. When it looks like wet scrambled eggs, stir in the calcium sulfate and cook for another minute, then turn off the heat. Let it cool to below 100°F.

Stir in the culture, transfer to a sterilized container with a lid, and put in a warm place at around 95°F for 16 to 24 hours, until it has reached a pH of between 4.5 and 4.9. Stir in the salt.

CONTINUED

DOG-GONE GOODA

CONTINUED

Line a sieve with a sterilized piece of cheesecloth (see page 21) and set over a bowl. Pour the curds into the cheesecloth and let drain for 4 to 6 hours, until you have 18 to 19 ounces (510g to 540g) of curds. (Don't discard the whey—save it to make "Whey to Go" Slicing Cheese on page 127—but it should be refrigerated or frozen if not used within 2 weeks.)

Now line a sterilized cheese mold or container of choice large enough to hold the curds with clean cheesecloth large enough to overhang. Pack and press the curds into the mold. Cover the top with the cheesecloth and refrigerate for a day.

Remove the cheese from the mold and the cheesecloth and wrap it in parchment paper. Put the cheese in the refrigerator and let it age for 4 to 8 weeks, until firm and sliceable. Once it is firm, you can wrap it in plastic wrap to keep it longer, up to 2 months, or coat in wax (see How to Wax Cheese, page 38) to keep it for months or up to 2 years.

FETA FETISH

MAKES ABOUT 1 POUND (450G)

3 cups (710ml) water

1 cup (140g) watermelon seed kernels (see Resources, page 201)

½ cup (70g) hemp hearts

½ cup (70g) almonds

½ cup (110g) refined or deodorized cocoa butter, shea butter, or coconut oil, melted

1 teaspoon fine sea salt, plus 1 tablespoon or more as needed for coating the cheese

1 teaspoon calcium sulfate

¼ teaspoon vegan thermophilic culture

BRINE

Whey, from draining

3 tablespoons sea salt

1 tablespoon distilled white vinegar, if needed to lower pH

High in protein, and a bit grassy and briny in flavor with a crumbly texture, this ode to feta is the perfect topping for salads or baked in a spanakopita. Feta comes in many styles in different parts of the Mediterranean, ranging from soft to firm, creamy to crumbly, and with even different degrees of saltiness. This rendition allows you to adapt it to your liking, making it firm and crumbly or softer and creamier, depending on how you age and preserve it.

IN A BLENDER, combine the water, watermelon seed kernels, hemp hearts, almonds, melted cocoa butter, and 1 teaspoon sea salt and process until as smooth as possible, 1 to 2 minutes. Pour this mixture into a nut milk bag, squeezing to extract as much milk as possible into a medium saucepan. (Reserve the pulp for another use; see pages 183 to 199.)

Set the saucepan over medium heat and bring to a simmer, scraping the coagulated curds from the sides and bottom slowly and frequently. When it has mostly curdled, stir in the calcium sulfate, which will help solidify the curds even more.

Let this mixture cool until it is below 110°F. Stir in the culture. Put it in a sterilized container large enough to hold the cheese and then set it in a warm place where it will maintain a temperature between 95° and 105°F for 16 to 24 hours, until it reaches a pH of 4.6 or slightly below.

Place a sieve or ricotta mold over a bowl or container and line it with a large piece of cheesecloth. Pour the curds into this to drain the whey into the container below (reserve the whey for the brine).

Cover the top of the curds with the cheesecloth hanging down, and place a heavy weight on it—a large, clean stone, heavy pot filled with water, or whatever you can find that will work—and allow the weight to press the cheese for 6 to 8 hours.

When the cheese is firm enough to hold its shape, remove the cheesecloth and sprinkle it very generously on all sides with the

CONTINUED

FETA FETISH

CONTINUED

1 tablespoon salt. Put the whey in the refrigerator until later, and place the cheese back in the sieve over an empty bowl, or on a cooling rack (for baking), and let it dry at room temperature for a full 1 to 2 days until it is very firm; the salt will help to evaporate the moisture.

Make the brine: After a couple of days, when the cheese is very dry and firm, take the whey out of the fridge. Measure it and add water to bring it to 2 cups. Heat the whey/water mixture with the salt and stir well to dissolve. Add the vinegar and allow it to cool (this can be made a day or two earlier as well).

When the cheese is firm, cut it into large cubes or 1-inch slices and put it into a storage container big enough to fit it and all the brine.

Store the cheese in the brine, making sure it is fully submerged in it, in the refrigerator, where it will keep for 6 to 8 weeks. It will get stronger in flavor and saltier over time. Alternatively, after brining the cheese for a week in the refrigerator, you can drain it and cover it in olive oil, where it will keep for 2 to 3 months. The cheese will be richer and not as salty or funky.

 NOTE

If your feta is not as tangy as you like, add ¼ to ½ teaspoon of citric acid to the brine. After a day or two, it should get tangier.

HIGH SIERRA ALPINE-STYLE CHEESE

MAKES 1 POUND (450G)

1 cup (140g) watermelon seed kernels (see Resources, page 201)

Generous ¾ cup (120g) almonds

½ cup (140g) pumpkin seeds

4 cups (950ml) water

½ cup (110g) deodorized or natural shea butter, melted

1 teaspoon fine sea salt

1 teaspoon calcium sulfate

3 tablespoons shio-kōji

¼ teaspoon vegan thermophilic culture, such as Kazu

⅛ teaspoon Propionic shermanii (optional; helps with creation of gas that leads to hole formation)

BRINE

1 quart (1L) water

¼ cup (70g) fine sea salt

This cheese was the result of another experiment that shocked me six weeks later, when I finally cut into the wheel. Rough-looking curds had melted into a smooth, waxy, pliable cheese with little holes reminiscent of an Alpine-style cheese. The flavor was mild with a nutty note and a nice rind.

IN A BLENDER, combine the watermelon seed kernels, almonds, pumpkin seeds, water, melted shea butter, and salt and process on high speed until smooth and creamy. Pour the mixture into a nut milk bag and squeeze to extract as much milk as possible into a medium saucepan. (Reserve the pulp for another use; see pages 183 to 199.)

Set the saucepan over medium heat and bring to a simmer, occasionally scraping the sides and bottom until you begin to see some curds begin to form. Add the calcium sulfate and continue to cook until the entire mass has turned into soft, milky curds.

Pour the curds into a sterilized 1-quart (1L) jar and refrigerate for a couple of hours until it has cooled down to 85° to 90°F. Stir in the shio-kōji, culture, and Propionic shermanii (if using).

Cover the jar and put it in a warm place where it can maintain a temperature of 85° to 90°F for 16 to 20 hours. If you have used Propionic shermanii, aim for a pH of around 5.7 to 6.0. If not, aim for a lower pH, between 4.6 and 5.0.

Line a sieve with sterilized cheesecloth (see page 21) set over a bowl and pour the cultured cheese into it. Allow it to drain in the refrigerator for 24 hours.

On the third day, you will form the cheese and prepare it for long aging. Line a cheese mold of choice or 6-inch (15cm) round cake pan with clean cheesecloth, leaving enough overhang to fold over. Put the drained curds into the mold and press to form a wheel, and fold the overhang over the top of the cheese. Put this in the refrigerator overnight. The next day, take the cheesecloth-wrapped cheese out

CONTINUED

HIGH SIERRA ALPINE-STYLE CHEESE

of the mold and set it on a cooling rack in the refrigerator to firm up for 1 week to 10 days.

Make the brine: In a saucepan, combine the water and salt. Bring to a boil, stirring to dissolve the salt. Allow to cool briefly, then pour the brine into a sterilized glass or plastic container large enough to hold the wheel of cheese. Refrigerate the brine until cool.

Remove the cheese from the refrigerator and unwrap the cheesecloth. Submerge the cheese wheel in the brine and refrigerate for 24 hours. Remove the cheese and let it dry on a cooling rack for several hours at room temperature.

Wrap the cheese loosely in parchment paper and return it to age in the refrigerator for another 4 to 6 weeks, until it is fully hard and sliceable. The cheese inside will be hard but pliable, and if you're lucky, have little holes. You can also age it, unwrapped, in which case a light rind will form.

Store the aged cheese wrapped in cheese paper or plastic wrap in the refrigerator for 2 to 3 months. To keep it longer, wax it (see How to Wax Cheese, page 38); it will then keep for 1 to 2 years and get better and better over time.

PARMACASIO

MAKES ABOUT 1½ POUNDS (680G)

2 cups (280g) cashews

¾ cup (180ml) water

½ cup (120ml) olive brine

⅔ cup (33g) nutritional yeast flakes

½ cup (110g) deodorized cocoa butter, melted

¼ cup (55g) deodorized shea butter or refined coconut oil, melted

¾ cup (90g) chickpea flour

1½ ounces (50g) pitted green olives

2 tablespoons (60g) white miso

1½ teaspoons fine sea salt, plus more for sprinkling

¼ teaspoon vegan thermophilic culture

2 tablespoons shio-kōji

About ¼ cup (55g) deodorized cocoa butter (optional; for coating), melted

Parmigiano-Reggiano comes from Parma, Italy, and Parmacasio comes from my humble kitchen in Nicasio, California. It's a great substitute for Parmesan for grating on pasta, for enriching sauces and soups, and for adding a sharp, umami-filled kick.

IN A SAUCEPAN, combine the cashews with water to cover. Bring to a boil and boil for about 5 minutes (this is done to ensure that the cashews are pasteurized). Drain well.

In a blender, combine the drained cashews, the ¾ cup (180ml) water, and the olive brine and process until smooth and creamy. Add the nutritional yeast, melted cocoa butter, shea butter, chickpea flour, olives, miso, and salt and process until smooth and creamy. Make sure that the mixture is no higher in temperature than 110°F; otherwise, let it cool.

Add the culture and stir well. Transfer to a sterilized container and put in a warm place where it can maintain a temperature of between 100° and 110°F for 24 to 36 hours, until it reaches a pH of 5.0 to 5.2.

After culturing, stir in the shio-kōji and mix well. Line a mold with a clean piece of cheesecloth and pack in the cheese, smoothing the top. Put this in the refrigerator overnight or longer to firm up.

Remove the cheesecloth and place the wheel on a cheese mat over a cooling rack (for air circulation). If you want a light, dry rind, use a salt shaker to sprinkle the entire surface liberally with salt. If you prefer no dry rind, you can first coat the cheese with a light coating of melted coconut oil or cocoa butter and then sprinkle liberally with salt. Either way, the salt will discourage mold growth.

Put the rack with the cheese into a wine fridge or refrigerator and let it age for 8 to 12 weeks, until firm and dry. You can continue to age it, and it will develop a more robust flavor and continue to dry out.

Store the aged cheese wrapped in cheese paper or parchment and then in a plastic bag in the refrigerator for 6 months or longer, but be sure to check the moisture level every month or so. If it starts to dry out too much so that it is difficult to slice with a sharp knife, wax it (see How to Wax Cheese, page 38). In wax, it can age for 2 to 3 years.

SMOKED PROVOLONE

MAKES ABOUT 12 OUNCES (340G)

1 cup (140g) watermelon seed kernels (see Resources, page 201)

2 cups (600ml) water

3 tablespoons nutritional yeast flakes

⅓ cup (75g) unsweetened nondairy yogurt, store-bought or homemade, such as Thick Oat-Cashew Yogurt (page 86), Watermelon Seed Kernel Milk Yogurt (page 89), Soy Yogurt (page 83), or Rich Soy-Cashew Yogurt (page 85)

4 tablespoons (55ml) avocado oil or other neutral vegetable oil

¼ cup (40g) tapioca starch

2 teaspoons psyllium husk powder

½ teaspoon lactic acid

2 teaspoons fine sea salt

5 teaspoons agar-agar powder

About ¼ cup wood chips, for smoking

This cheese is truly smoked—on your stovetop! Even if you don't have a stovetop smoker, you can convert your Dutch oven into one. The type of wood chip you choose will determine how smoky the cheese is, with hickory producing the smokiest results, while woods like maple will yield a more delicate smoke flavor. It makes a pleasant snacking cheese with crackers and is great in hot and cold sandwiches with a vegan meat alternative or even pan-fried eggplant. It's extremely sliceable with a nice dark, smoky rind giving way to a beautiful white interior that's soft, creamy, and pliable.

This smoked provolone is based on Fresh Watermelon Seed Kernel Mozzarella (page 115) with a few tweaks, but the processing and aging time are what differentiate it.

IN A BLENDER, process the watermelon seed kernels to a powder. Add 2 cups (480ml) of the water and the nutritional yeast and process to make a creamy milk, scraping the blender jar if needed to make sure no seeds are stuck on the sides. Pour the mixture into a nut milk bag and strain into a pot.

Set the pot over medium heat and cook, scraping the bottom slowly and regularly to lift the curds; they should be large. Cook until the pot is mostly curds with some milky whey bubbling up, 8 to 10 minutes. Pour through a sieve set over a bowl, reserving the whey.

In a blender, combine the curds, yogurt, oil, tapioca starch, psyllium powder, lactic acid, and salt and process until smooth. Oil a round cheese mold or bowl of choice large enough to hold the cheese and have at the ready.

In a medium pot, dissolve the agar in the remaining whey. Cover and bring to a boil over medium heat. Pour this quickly into the other ingredients in the blender and process briefly. Then pour this back into the pot and cook, whisking almost constantly, until very, very thick, gooey, and stretchy.

Pour the cheese into the oiled mold and refrigerate for several hours until firm. Take it out of the mold, wrap loosely in cheesecloth, and place on a cooling rack in your refrigerator or wine fridge for 4 to 7 days to let it dry out. You want the cheese to be somewhat dry before you smoke it so that it doesn't melt into a puddle.

To smoke the cheese, place the cheese on a rack in a stovetop smoker, or make one yourself by using a Dutch oven or other sturdy pot. Grab the wood chips, run some water over them, and place them at the bottom of the smoker or Dutch oven. If using a smoker, it'll likely come with a rack, so put the cheese on that. Otherwise, put the cheese in a small colander and place in the pot. Cover the smoker or pot and turn on the heat. After you smell the smoke, turn the heat to low and set the timer for about 30 minutes—beyond that and the cheese will start to melt. Remove the cheese from the smoker and allow to cool completely in the refrigerator.

Wrap the cheese in cheesecloth and place on a rack (for air circulation) in the refrigerator or wine fridge and age for 1 to 3 weeks. After this time, remove the cheesecloth and the cheese is ready to eat. The longer you age it, the firmer it will be.

SNOW WHITE RIND

MAKES ONE 8-OUNCE (225G) WHEEL

1 cup (140g) almonds (if not using a high-powered blender, soak in water for 8 hours, then drain and rinse)

½ cup (70g) pumpkin seeds

½ cup (70g) hemp hearts

3 cups (710ml) water

1½ teaspoons calcium sulfate dissolved in 1 tablespoon water

1 teaspoon fine sea salt

⅛ teaspoon vegan mesophilic culture

⅛ teaspoon MinusMilk (vegan version of Flora Danica; see Resources, page 201)

A small pinch (¹⁄₃₂ teaspoon) Penicillium candidum

A very small pinch (¹⁄₆₄ teaspoon) Geotrichum candidum (optional)

Mold Spray (recipe follows), optional but encouraged

I made my first vegan version of a bloomy rind cheese (aka Brie or Camembert) about fifteen years ago. I used cashews then, as I did for many cheeses. My issue was that the cheeses never became softer or runnier even as they "ripened" as their animal dairy counterparts do.

In playing around with various milk combinations, I found that I was able to produce a bloomy rind that became stronger and runnier over time, much as with animal milk. This has become my "go-to" milk for bloomy rind cheeses now as well as for The Barn (page 154), another cheese that changes textures over time.

Making bloomy rinds is an art and takes practice. Everything from moisture content and pH of the cheese to the humidity and ambient temperature are critical for success.

IN A BLENDER, combine the almonds, pumpkin seeds, hemp hearts, and water and blend until smooth and milky, 1 to 2 minutes. Pour this mixture through a nut milk bag and squeeze to extract as much milk out as possible into a saucepan. (Reserve the pulp for another use; see pages 183 to 199.)

Set the saucepan over medium-low heat and bring to a simmer, scraping the sides and bottom occasionally. When the milk has begun to form very light curds and reached a temperature of over 185°F, add the dissolved calcium sulfate and mix into the milk; continue to cook for 15 seconds. Put the pan in the refrigerator and let it cool and coagulate until it has cooled to below 90°F, 1 to 2 hours.

Stir in ½ teaspoon of the salt, the culture, MinusMilk, the Penicillium candidum, and Geotrichum candidum (if using). If you have a cheese mold designed for draining with lots of holes, you can sterilize it and place it over a jar or other container so that the whey can drain below. Otherwise, using a rubber band, attach a large, sterilized piece of cheesecloth (see page 21) over a wide-mouth jar or deep dish. Pour the cheese into the cheesecloth so that the whey can drain below. Put the jar in a warm place where it can maintain a temperature of around 85°F for 16 to 20 hours, until a pH of 4.5 to 4.6 is reached.

Before ripening the cheese and letting the mold grow, first check that the cheese is adequately firm. It should feel springy to the touch. If it is still wet, take the cheese out of the mold, wrap it in a few layers of cheesecloth or paper towels, and put it in the refrigerator for 8 to 24 hours, changing the towels as they get wet.

Get your ripening box (see page 36) ready. A Japanese bamboo sushi mat is good for bloomy rinds, and if made properly, the mold will inhabit the bamboo and make future batches easier to make. You can also use a cheese mat. Place the mat in the ripening box.

If the cheese was drained in a cheese mold, unmold the cheese, sprinkle with the remaining ½ teaspoon salt, and place on the sushi mat. If it was drained in hanging cheesecloth, line a mold with plastic wrap, pack the cheese in it, and press to form a wheel. Unmold the cheese, sprinkle with the remaining ½ teaspoon salt, and place on the mat in the box.

Spray the cheese lightly with mold spray. Although spraying is optional, I find it encourages mold growth. Cover the box with cheesecloth (not the lid) and keep at room temperature for 24 to 36 hours; this will allow the cheese to continue drying and help prevent a wet surface.

Carefully flip the cheese and spray. This time, cover the ripening box with a lid and keep at room temperature for another 2 to 3 days, flipping and spraying lightly daily, until you see mold growth. The humidity in the box should be around 91%; if you begin to see beads of water accumulate in the box or the surface of the cheese, blot with a clean paper towel; you may need to remove the lid and re-cover with cheesecloth to allow the cheese to dry out a bit more.

Once the mold starts to take root, you can flip every 2 days. In winter, I can generally keep the cheese in a cool spot inside until the entire surface is covered in mold (7 to 10 days). In the summer, I will only keep at room temperature for 2 to 4 days until I see mold growth, then will move it to a wine fridge. Note that the cooler the temperature, the slower the mold growth will be.

Once the mold has covered most of the surface of the cheese, you can move the cheese to your refrigerator. If the mold starts to look fuzzy, just pat it down. After the mold has covered the cheese entirely, you

CONTINUED

can wrap the cheese if you want (although it's not necessary) or just keep it in the container. If you choose to wrap it, use a cheese paper designed for bloomy rind cheeses or parchment paper, as the mold needs oxygen to survive.

Store in the refrigerator for 6 to 8 weeks. It will get stronger in flavor as it ripens and ages.

Mold Spray

Bring ½ cup (120ml) water to a boil, then let it cool to room temperature. Pour into a small glass spray bottle and add ¼ teaspoon Penicillium candidum, a pinch of salt, and a pinch of Geotrichum candidum.

White Ash Rind

Coating the surface of Snow White Rind (page 150) in activated charcoal helps to alkalize the surface, encouraging mold growth, and it looks beautiful as well. After salting your wheel, sprinkle some activated charcoal on the surface of the cheese and follow the directions above for ripening.

White Mountain Goat

This is a "goat" cheese covered in *Penicillium candidum,* reminding me of the white goats I saw on the snowy steppes of Mt. Etna.

MAKE REGGIE GOAT (page 105) and follow the directions for Snow White Rind (page 150) for ripening and growing the mold.

THE BARN, A STINKY CHEESE

MAKES 12 OUNCES (340G)

1 cup (140g) almonds (soak in water for 8 hours if not using a high-powered blender)

½ cup (70g) pumpkin seeds

½ cup (70g) hemp hearts

3 cups (710ml) water

½ teaspoon citric acid, or 1½ teaspoons calcium sulfate

⅛ teaspoon vegan mesophilic culture

A small pinch (1⁄32 teaspoon) Penicillium candidum

A small pinch (1⁄32 teaspoon) Geotrichum candidum

A small pinch (1⁄32 teaspoon) Brevibacterium linens

½ teaspoon salt

BRINE

1 cup (240ml) hot water

2 tablespoons fine sea salt

1 tablespoon distilled white vinegar

A small pinch (1⁄32 teaspoon) Geotrichum candidum

A small pinch (1⁄32 teaspoon) Brevibacterium linens

A barn filled with the smell of goats, sheep, and wet straw can either turn you on or off—I happen to be one who loves those earthy smells. Likewise, a cheese like Limburger is worse than stinky socks to some, while eliciting joy in others. I fall into the second camp and am always delighted when I meet others who appreciate them, too.

These stinky cheeses are called washed rind cheeses because they are washed with a brine inoculated with bacteria that create the classic orange rind and break down fats and proteins, yielding their strong, stinky flavor. If you like strong, stinky, gooey cheeses, this one is for you.

IN A BLENDER, combine the almonds, pumpkin seeds, hemp hearts, and water. Process on high speed until as creamy as possible, about a minute. Pour the mixture into a nut milk bag and squeeze to extract as much milk as possible into a medium saucepan. (Reserve the pulp for another use; see pages 183 to 199.)

Set the saucepan over medium-low heat and bring to a simmer. Using a silicone spatula, scrape the bottom and sides occasionally as curds form. When it starts to simmer around the edges or reaches 200°F, add the citric acid or calcium sulfate and stir gently. Turn off the heat and allow the mixture to sit for an hour or so until the temperature falls to below 90°F.

Stir in the culture, Penicillium candidum, Geotrichum candidum, and Brevibacterium linens. Transfer to a sterilized container, cover, and put in a warm place where it can maintain a temperature of around 90°F for 12 to 16 hours, to reach a pH of between 4.5 and 4.9.

After the desired pH has been reached, line a sieve with sterilized cheesecloth (see page 21) and place it over a wide-mouth jar or bowl. Pour the cheese over the cheesecloth to allow the whey to drain. Refrigerate for 24 hours until it looks like a firm ricotta and has a springy texture. Stir in the salt.

Make the brine: This can be done at any time before the second day. In a clean jar, combine the hot water, salt, and vinegar and stir until most of the salt is dissolved. Let cool to below 95°F, then add the Geotrichum candidum and Brevibacterium linens. Set aside to use for the next few days.

After 24 hours, the cheese should be firm enough to form. To form into a wheel, line a mold with plastic wrap and press into a wheel shape, then turn out of the mold onto a sterilized cheese mat. Or roll into a log, using plastic wrap to help you form the log. Then remove the plastic wrap and set the log on a sterilized cheese mat.

Set the cheese mat in a ripening box (see page 36). Using a pastry brush, brush the surface of the cheese with the brine (this is called "washing the rind"). Cover with a lid and keep at room temperature for a day.

On the second day, open the ripening box and wipe down any heavy moisture that has accumulated in it. Now flip the cheese and "wash" it again with the brine. Continue this procedure, flipping and washing the surface, every day for 3 to 4 days until you see some orange.

Depending on the season, if it is winter and cold, I will let the cheese ripen at room temperature for the first 3 or 4 days, then move to the refrigerator. In summer, I will start at room temperature, then move to a wine fridge or refrigerator after 36 to 48 hours. You need high moisture to encourage the growth of Brevibacterium linens, so some beads of moisture in the box are fine, but too much will make the surface of the cheese wet, so be sure to wipe down the box from excess moisture each day. The surface of the cheese should be moist and feel tacky, but not wet or completely slippery.

You should start seeing an orange rind in a week or two depending on conditions, humidity, and temperature. The cheese itself will change in texture to soft and gooey over the next 2 to 8 weeks. You can wrap in cheese paper after the rind has developed. The flavor will become funkier and stronger over time, as the proteins and fats break down. I have kept this cheese for up to 2 months in the refrigerator.

RANCHO ROCKFORT

MAKES 12 OUNCES (340G)

1⅔ cups (250g) pumpkin seeds

¾ cup (105g) hemp hearts

3¾ cups (900ml) water

½ cup (110g) refined coconut oil, melted

3 teaspoons fine sea salt

¼ teaspoon vegan mesophilic culture

¹⁄₁₆ teaspoon vegan Penicillium roqueforti

As I mentioned earlier, the story of the first Roquefort is one of love: A shepherd saw a beautiful lass, so he tucked his piece of cheese behind a rock and left to pursue her. When he returned to retrieve his cheese, it was covered in blue mold. I have to say that my own experimentation with blue cheese was a little like this: I tucked mine away in my little "cave"—a wine fridge—and crossed my fingers my love would be requited, and lo and behold—it was!

It is an art form, however, and there are many nuances to producing the perfect blue. And then again, what's "perfect" is in the eye (or taste buds) of the beholder, as some blues are pungent and strong, while others are milder and more buttery. There are so many nuances to making blue cheese that we need to be patient about learning what tastes best to us. Even the blue mold cultures themselves differ in strength and type of flavor, and then the process itself, such as how many holes you poke in the cheese (the more holes you poke for the mold to grow, the stronger the cheese), as well as how long you let it ripen or age, will all affect the results. Of all the cheeses in this book, this and the following one, Nicasio Blues (page 160), are the most challenging.

But let me reassure you that if you follow these directions carefully, you will get some sort of blue cheese. How strong, how mild, how pungent it will be—you will arrive at your enlightened wheel of blue with practice.

IN A BLENDER, combine the pumpkin seeds, hemp hearts, water, coconut oil, and 2 teaspoons of the salt and process until smooth and creamy. Pour the mixture through a nut milk bag into a saucepan. (Reserve the pulp for another use; see pages 183 to 199.)

Set the saucepan over medium heat and cook, scraping the bottom and sides with a silicone spatula occasionally and gently as large curds form as it comes to a simmer. Do not use a whisk, and do not

CONTINUED

overscrape, as you want to keep the curds as large as possible. Continue doing this for several minutes until mostly clear whey bubbles up between the curds. The whole process should take 10 to 15 minutes.

Line a sieve with sterilized cheesecloth (see page 21) and set over a bowl. Pour the mixture into the sieve and allow most of the whey to drain, about 20 minutes. The curds should still be very moist.

Transfer the curds to a sterilized bowl. If the curds are very dry, add a cup or so of the whey back into them (they need moisture for effective fermentation). Allow the curds to cool to 80°F.

Using a sterilized spoon, stir in the culture and Penicillium roqueforti. Line a cheese mold with sterilized cheesecloth and transfer the curds to the mold, making sure that they are still moist. Put the mold on a wire rack with a pan underneath to catch the whey as it drains. Cover the mold with plastic wrap or a lid. Put the cheese where it can maintain a temperature of 80° to 90°F for 14 to 24 hours, or until it reaches a pH of 4.6 to 5.2.

When it has reached the proper pH, press the cheese gently to extract the remaining whey but not enough to render the cheese as one solid mass (you want to leave the slightest bit of space between the curds for mold growth). Transfer the cheese to the refrigerator to firm up overnight.

Gently unmold the cheese and remove the cheesecloth. The cheese will look very lumpy but should hold together as one piece. Sprinkle the surface of the cheese all over with the remaining 1 teaspoon salt. Use a bamboo skewer or thermometer rod and poke around 20 holes in the cheese almost to the bottom. This is so that the mold can reach the inside (there should also be some separation between the curds if you have not pressed the cheese too much).

Put a sterilized cheese mat on top of a cheese rack or several layers of paper towels inside a ripening box (see page 36). Place the cheese on the mat in the box and cover it with a lid. Put the box in a wine fridge or a refrigerator and flip the cheese every day for about 4 days in a wine fridge or 10 to 14 days in a refrigerator, at which point you should see a little blue mold growth.

Continue to flip the cheese every 2 days until the cheese is mostly covered in mold and the blue flavor develops, 2 to 3 weeks in a wine fridge and 3 to 4 in a refrigerator (mold growth is slowed when temperatures fall below 52°F). If the humidity rises too high and you see beads of water accumulating in the box, wipe it out with a paper towel (the humidity should be between 85% and 92%). You may also see white or orange mold growth; if you do, immediately scrape it off with a clean knife.

At this point, you can scrape off most of the blue mold on the exterior of the cheese to prevent the flavor from becoming too strong and ammoniated over time (some people prefer not to do this). Take a clean skewer and poke another 10 to 15 holes in the cheese. Now wrap the cheese in aluminum foil. You will continue to age the cheese in the foil. The aluminum foil limits oxygen to the surface, which prevents excessive or unwanted mold growth, while allowing the mold to reach the interior of the cheese due to the holes that were poked.

Once the cheese is fully ripe and veins have formed inside (you can determine this by tasting it), the cheese will keep, wrapped in the aluminum foil, for a month or even longer. The longer it stores, the stronger the flavor will get.

NICASIO BLUES

**MAKES ABOUT 1 POUND
(450G)**

5 cups (1.2L) water

Scant 2¼ cups (300g)
pumpkin seeds

Scant 1 cup (125g) hemp
hearts

¾ cup (100g) watermelon
seed kernels (see Resources,
page 201)

½ cup (105g) refined coconut
oil, melted

½ cup (105g) refined shea
butter, melted

2 tablespoons white or
light miso

1 tablespoon shio-kōji

⅔ cup (33g) nutritional yeast
flakes

2 teaspoons fine sea salt

¼ teaspoon vegan mesophilic
culture

¹⁄₁₆ teaspoon vegan Penicillium
roqueforti

Annatto, for color, as needed

The base of this cheese is firmer and more robust in flavor than Rancho Rockfort (page 156). It also ages nicely, and for some reason, it doesn't seem to get as funky in flavor over time as Rancho Rockfort.

IN A BLENDER, combine the water, pumpkin seeds, hemp hearts, watermelon seed kernels, coconut oil, shea butter, miso, shio-kōji, nutritional yeast, and 1 teaspoon of the salt and process on high speed until creamy, 1 to 2 minutes. Pour the mixture into a nut milk bag and squeeze to extract as much milk as possible into a saucepan. (Reserve the pulp for another use; see pages 183 to 199.)

Set the pan over medium heat, and as the milk heats up, it will begin to curdle on the bottom. Use a silicone spatula to scrape the bottom and sides slowly and gently to move the curds, but not to disturb them too much. Do not stir or whisk as that will break the curds; simply scrape gently and slowly to lift the curds and allow new curds to form as they heat. When it is done, it will look like scrambled eggs in a milky sauce.

Pour the curds and whey into a sterilized bowl and allow to cool to 90°F or lower. Stir in the culture and Penicillium roqueforti. Cover the bowl and put it in a warm place between 85° and 90°F until it reaches a pH of 4.6 or slightly below, 16 to 20 hours.

Line a sieve or a cheese mold made for draining with a large piece of sterilized cheesecloth (see page 21). Place the sieve over a bowl and pour the cheese into it. Allow to drain for 4 to 8 hours, until almost completely dry (there may not be a lot of whey).

Transfer the drained curds to a food processor and process until creamy. Line a mold with plastic wrap or sterilized cheesecloth and pack in the cheese. Transfer the mold to the refrigerator and allow it to firm up overnight.

Remove the cheese from the mold, peel off the plastic wrap, and sprinkle the entire surface with the remaining 1 teaspoon salt. Set the cheese on a sterilized cheese mat. Using a clean skewer, poke the cheese on the top and sides about 30 times, then place in a ripening box (see page 36). Put the box in a wine fridge or a refrigerator and flip the cheese every day for about 4 days in a wine fridge or 10 to 14 days in a refrigerator, at which point you should see a little blue mold growth.

Continue to flip the cheese every 2 days until the cheese is mostly covered in mold, 2 to 3 weeks in a wine fridge and 3 to 4 weeks in a refrigerator. If you see beads of water inside the ripening box, wipe it down with a paper towel to control the humidity. You may also see white or orange mold growth; if you do, immediately scrape it off with a clean knife.

When the entire surface is covered in blue mold, scrape most of it off. Take a clean skewer and poke another 10 to 15 holes in the cheese. Now wrap the cheese in aluminum foil. You will continue to age the cheese in the foil. The aluminum foil limits oxygen to the surface, which prevents excessive or unwanted mold growth, while allowing the mold to reach the interior of the cheese due to the holes that were poked.

Once the cheese is fully ripe and veins have formed inside (you can determine this by tasting it), the cheese will keep, wrapped in the aluminum foil, for a month or even longer. The longer it stores, the stronger the flavor will get.

CHAPTER 6

Ice Cream
and Gelato

A rich, creamy mouthfeel that lingers in your mouth as it melts—that's what we want in ice cream. Vegan ice creams have come a long way over the past decade, but many achieve this creamy mouthfeel from either added oils or coconut milk that can sometimes overpower other flavors. My challenge was to create an ice cream or gelato base that would deliver that rich mouthfeel without coconut milk or added oils. In this chapter, I present three healthy options for an ice cream base that are neutral in flavor and rich in texture, with the hope that it will inspire you to create your own exciting flavors.

To churn or not to churn—I am partial to churning my ice cream in an ice cream maker because I love that just-churned soft texture. For those who don't have ice cream makers, however, the first two bases work almost as well by simply pouring into a container and freezing. In addition, the flavors with alcohol in them also remain creamy when just frozen without churning.

TWO CASHEW ICE CREAM BASES

Rich cashew milk combined with either cooked rice or oats creates that round mouthfeel of ice creams made with full-fat heavy cream without the addition of oil.

Cashew-Rice Ice Cream Base

MAKES ABOUT 1 QUART (1L)

2½ cups (600ml) water

1 cup (140g) cashews

1 cup cooked white rice (130g to 180g), preferably medium- or short-grain

½ cup (100g) organic sugar or (120ml) maple syrup

Using up leftover cooked rice couldn't get better! However, note two things: The weight of cooked rice varies depending on whether it is short-, medium-, or long-grain; hence it's best to measure this volumetrically rather than by weight. And if your leftover rice is very dry from being refrigerated, steam for a few minutes or sprinkle with a couple of tablespoons of water and microwave to rehydrate and soften, or it will be difficult to puree into a cream and you'll end up with hard bits of rice.

IN A BLENDER, combine the water, cashews, rice, and sugar and process until absolutely smooth and creamy and no kernels of rice are visible or palpable, 2 to 3 minutes. You can now use this to make ice cream.

Cashew-Oat Ice Cream Base

MAKES ABOUT 1 QUART (1L)

3 cups (710ml) water

1½ cups (210g) cashews

½ cup (120ml) coconut milk

½ cup (100g) organic sugar or
(120ml) maple syrup

¼ cup (25g) rolled oats

If you don't have leftover rice and don't feel like cooking any, fear not—oats and a bit of coconut milk work well. If you don't like coconut, that's also not a worry because you won't be able to taste it—the coconut just provides a bit of richness. This base must be cooked to activate the starch in the cashews and to thicken the oats, both of which contribute to a rich and creamy mouthfeel.

IN A BLENDER, combine the water, cashews, coconut milk, sugar, and oats and process for a minute or two until smooth and creamy. Pour into a saucepan and cook over medium heat, stirring frequently with a whisk and occasionally scraping the sides and bottom with a silicone spatula, until it is thick like gravy. Allow to cool to room temperature before using to make ice cream.

VANILLA THYME GELATO

MAKES ABOUT 1 QUART (1L)

4 cups (950ml) Cashew-Rice Ice Cream Base (page 166) or Cashew-Oat Ice Cream Base (page 167)

2 tablespoons fresh thyme

2 teaspoons vanilla extract

1 large or 2 small vanilla beans (when in doubt, you can use a little more!)

One of my favorite flavor combinations, this is surprisingly fabulous, usually eliciting "wows" from guests.

IN A BLENDER, combine the ice cream base, thyme, and vanilla extract. Cut the vanilla bean lengthwise to open and scrape the seeds into the blender. Blitz for 10 to 20 seconds to "mince" the thyme but not turn the ice cream green. Freeze in a plastic container or churn in an ice cream maker, following the manufacturer's instructions.

COFFEE KAHLÚA CRUNCH GELATO

MAKES ABOUT 1 QUART (1L)

3 cups (710ml) Cashew-Rice Ice Cream Base (page 166) or Cashew-Oat Ice Cream Base (page 167)

½ cup (120ml) espresso or very strong coffee

½ cup (120ml) Kahlúa

¼ cup (50g) organic sugar

½ cup (120g) cacao nibs

Cacao nibs add a delightful crunch to a classic coffee ice cream made more sophisticated with a generous splash of Kahlúa. If you want to skip the alcohol, simply increase the espresso by another ¼ cup.

IN A BLENDER, combine the ice cream base, espresso, Kahlúa, and sugar and process to combine well. Mix in the cacao nibs by hand and freeze in a plastic container or churn in an ice cream maker, following the manufacturer's instructions.

FRESH STRAWBERRY
(OR OTHER BERRY) ICE CREAM

MAKES ABOUT 1 QUART (1L)

12 ounces (340g) sliced fresh strawberries (or other berries, such as blackberries or raspberries)

¼ cup (50g) organic sugar

3 cups (710ml) Cashew-Rice Ice Cream Base (page 166) or Cashew-Oat Ice Cream Base (page 167)

Here's a great version of a good old classic. Feel free to use other berries, such as blackberries or raspberries, following the same method.

PUT THE STRAWBERRIES or other berries in a bowl and mix with the sugar. Let sit for 20 to 30 minutes to allow the juices to run out.

In a blender or food processor, process the berries (and juices) briefly to chop up but don't puree—leave a lot of little chunks.

Stir the strawberry mixture into the ice cream base and freeze in a plastic container or churn in an ice cream maker, following the manufacturer's instructions.

RUM RAISIN EGGNOG ICE CREAM

MAKES ABOUT 1 QUART (1L)

¾ cup (120g) raisins

1 cup (240ml) dark rum

¾ cup (150g) organic sugar

3 cups (710ml) Cashew-Rice Ice Cream Base (page 166, made with maple syrup)

¼ cup (60ml) maple syrup

2 teaspoons vanilla extract

1½ teaspoons freshly grated nutmeg

Rum raisin was my favorite flavor as a child who frequented Baskin-Robbins. I had to re-create it with this lush base and decided to enhance it with a bit of nutmeg for an eggnog flavor. It may now be my new favorite ice cream.

IN A SMALL saucepan, combine the raisins, rum, and sugar and bring to a simmer. Cook for 3 to 4 minutes to form a light syrup and allow the raisins to absorb the rum, making sure not to overcook to the point the syrup is too thick (much of the alcohol actually cooks off). Set a sieve over a bowl and pour the raisins into the sieve. Press the raisins with a wooden spoon to release more syrup.

In a blender, combine the ice cream base, the strained rum syrup, maple syrup, vanilla, and grated nutmeg and process briefly. Pour this into an ice cream maker and churn according to the manufacturer's instructions, adding the raisins after several minutes. (Alternatively, just pour into a container and freeze, but stir in the raisins only after partially freezing to make sure they don't all sink to the bottom.)

SALTED MAPLE CHOCOLATE CHIP COOKIE DOUGH ICE CREAM

MAKES ABOUT 1 QUART (1L)

3 cups (710ml) Cashew-Rice Ice Cream Base (page 166, made with maple syrup)

¼ cup (60g) maple syrup

¼ cup (50g) organic sugar

1 tablespoon vanilla extract

About 1 teaspoon flaky sea salt

1 cup (about 300g) dough from No-Waste Chocolate Chip Cookies (page 195) or other vegan chocolate chip cookie dough

Made with the dough from the chocolate chip cookies that use the pulp from milk recipes in this book with some flaky salt sprinkled throughout, this will surely become a favorite summertime treat for the family.

IN A BLENDER, combine the ice cream base, maple syrup, sugar, and vanilla and process until very smooth and creamy. Pour into an ice cream maker and begin to freeze, following the manufacturer's instructions. When it is semi-solid, add the flaky salt and continue to churn. Right before it's finished churning, drop heaping tablespoons of the cookie dough into the ice cream as it rotates, and let it turn only briefly (a few rotations) so that it is distributed throughout the ice cream but is not fully blended in. Serve right away or store in another container in the freezer.

WATERMELON SEED KERNEL MILK ICE CREAMS

I was delighted to find that high-protein watermelon seed kernel milk makes a rich and creamy ice cream base as well. No wonder, because it is an incredibly "milky" milk with a rich mouthfeel and will create a beautiful neutral base for whatever you dream up. If you have a cashew allergy or just want a boost of nutrition for dessert, this is the milk for you.

Although watermelon seed kernel milk is a great base on its own, for an extra boost in achieving that rich, round mouthfeel, add ½ to 1 cup cooked white rice—as in the Cashew-Rice Ice Cream Base, page 166—and blend until smooth. Don't try this with the oats, however, because watermelon seed kernel milk can curdle when heated.

Gianduja Gelato

MAKES ABOUT 5 CUPS (1.25L)

1¼ cups (175g) raw hazelnuts (see Note) or unsalted roasted hazelnuts

¾ cup (150g) organic sugar

3 ounces (85g) dark chocolate (70% to 80% cacao), melted

3 cups (710ml) Watermelon Seed Kernel Milk (page 54)

¾ cup (72g) unsweetened cocoa powder

2 teaspoons vanilla extract

This is an Italian favorite—a combination of chocolate with hazelnuts. Essentially, it's frozen Nutella gelato, and it's rich and indulgent.

IN A BLENDER, combine the hazelnuts, sugar, melted chocolate, and about ½ cup (120ml) of the watermelon seed kernel milk and process until smooth and creamy. Add the remaining milk and process until very creamy. Finally, add the cocoa powder and vanilla. Freeze in a plastic container or churn in an ice cream maker, following the manufacturer's instructions.

NOTE

If using raw hazelnuts, roast them: Preheat the oven to 325°F. Spread the hazelnuts on a sheet pan and roast until lightly browned but not dark, 12 to 15 minutes. Put the hazelnuts on a tea towel, fold the towel, and rub for about 30 seconds to remove as much of the skins as possible (the skins can be a bit bitter). If there are a few stubborn skins attached, it's not the end of the world.

Sorrentino Limoncello Gelato

MAKES 3 CUPS (750G)

2½ cups (600ml) Watermelon
Seed Kernel Milk (page 54)

¾ cup (150g) organic sugar

⅓ cup (80ml) limoncello

½ teaspoon grated lemon zest

¼ cup (60ml) fresh
lemon juice

This lovely treat will whisk you off to the scenic lemon-scented Amalfi Coast.

IN A BLENDER, combine the watermelon seed kernel milk, sugar, limoncello, lemon zest, and lemon juice and process for about 30 seconds, until blended. Freeze in a plastic container or churn in an ice cream maker, following the manufacturer's instructions; it'll be creamy either way.

Maple Ginger Cinnamon Gelato

MAKES ABOUT 1 QUART (1L)

3 cups (710ml) Watermelon
Seed Kernel Milk (page 54)

¾ cup (180ml) maple syrup

¼ cup (50g) organic sugar

1 tablespoon grated
fresh ginger

1 teaspoon ground cinnamon

I tried this flavor at an artisanal gelato shop in one of those quintessential little hilltop towns in Italy and loved it. It's a balanced, subtle blend of two spices, evoking the scents of the holiday season without being overpowering, making it perfect for any time of year.

IN A BLENDER, combine the watermelon seed kernel milk, maple syrup, sugar, ginger, and cinnamon and process for about 30 seconds, until blended. Freeze in a plastic container or churn in an ice cream maker, following the manufacturer's instructions.

(NOTE)

Puree the milk with ½ cup cooked white rice to provide a creamier base.

CONTINUED

Mango Mint Gelato

MAKES ABOUT 1 QUART (1L)

2 cups (470ml) Watermelon Seed Kernel Milk (page 54)

2 cups (370g) mango pieces, fresh or frozen

⅓ cup (65g) organic sugar

1½ teaspoons grated lemon zest

1 tablespoon coarsely chopped fresh mint leaves

A hint of mint added to mango creates an incredibly refreshing combination that's perfect as a summertime treat.

IN A BLENDER, combine the watermelon seed kernel milk, mango, sugar, and lemon zest and process until smooth. Add the mint and pulse a few times to mince but not to the point that the ice cream turns green. Freeze in a plastic container or churn in an ice cream maker, following the manufacturer's instructions. This gelato will be a bit icier if frozen overnight in a container; to make it creamy, you can process briefly in a food processor after it is frozen.

(NOTE)

Puree the milk with ½ cup cooked white rice to provide a creamier base.

CONTINUED

Mt. Etna Chocolate Cinnamon Café Gelato

MAKES ABOUT 1 QUART (1L)

3 cups (710ml) Watermelon Seed Kernel Milk (page 54)

4 tablespoons (20g) very finely ground dark coffee

½ cup (100g) organic sugar

½ cup (40g) unsweetened cocoa powder

3 ounces (85g) dark chocolate (70% to 80% cacao), melted

2 teaspoons vanilla extract

¼ teaspoon ground cinnamon

½ cup (120g) cacao nibs (optional)

Chocolate with cinnamon spiked with coffee is a great flavor combination found in many parts of the world, including Sicily, Mexico, and my home!

IN A BLENDER, combine the milk and ground coffee and blend until the mixture is a beautiful brown color. Line a sieve with cheesecloth set over a bowl and strain the milk to catch the finely ground coffee bits (if you want to skip this step, you can, but you will have a slightly grainy ice cream).

Return the milk to the blender and add the sugar, cocoa powder, melted chocolate, vanilla, and cinnamon and process again until smooth and creamy. Stir in the cacao nibs (if using), but don't blend. Freeze in a plastic container or churn in an ice cream maker, following the manufacturer's instructions.

CHAPTER 7

No-Waste Recipes and Other Favorites

A s you embark on your journey to make milk from nuts, seeds, and beans, you'll find yourself with leftover pulp and wonder what to do with it. Here at Rancho Compasión, I have the option of feeding some of the animals with it—but better yet, why not feed some humans by incorporating it into delicious upcycled recipes? And I guarantee that these recipes aren't just an excuse to use up leftovers but are truly wonderful on their own.

The No-Waste Crackers (page 189) will end up competing with the cheeses themselves (they have made me reconsider going back in business!). Never have I served them on a cheese board without someone remarking how wonderful they are. Then there's the Luscious Gluten-Free Salted Hazelnut Brownies (page 198) and the No-Waste Chocolate Chip Cookies (page 195)—the dough itself is just so addictively good! There are so many ways you can use leftover pulp, and I trust you'll come up with your own recipes. Leftover pulp makes a great staple ingredient that you can keep frozen for months and then thaw and use when needed, adding not only fiber and nutrition but great flavor.

NO-WASTE MOIST CARROT MUFFINS

MAKES 11 TO 12 MUFFINS

2 cups (about 200g) grated carrots

1 cup (about 185g) leftover pulp from making milk (almond, pumpkin seed, hemp, watermelon seed kernels, or any mixture; pages 44 to 54)

¾ cup (180ml) any nondairy milk, homemade (pages 44 to 54) or store-bought

½ cup (120ml) maple syrup

1½ teaspoons ground cinnamon

1 teaspoon ground ginger

¼ teaspoon ground cardamom

1½ cups (180g) whole wheat pastry flour

4 teaspoons baking powder

½ cup (60g) chopped walnuts, pistachios, pecans, or almonds (optional)

½ cup (80g) raisins (optional)

Using leftover nut milk pulp keeps these muffins sufficiently moist, so no oil is required. They are a tasty and super-healthy snack or breakfast treat.

PREHEAT THE OVEN to 350°F. Grease 11 to 12 cups of a muffin tin, or line with paper liners.

In a medium bowl, combine the carrots, leftover pulp, milk, maple syrup, cinnamon, ginger, and cardamom and mix well. In another bowl, whisk together the pastry flour and baking powder, then stir into the carrot/pulp mixture. Stir in the nuts and raisins, if using. Divide the batter among the muffin cups.

Bake until slightly risen, golden brown, and a toothpick inserted in the center of a muffin comes out clean, 25 to 30 minutes. Store wrapped in plastic wrap or in an airtight container in the refrigerator for a week.

NO-WASTE ITALIAN SAUSAGES AND SAUSAGE CRUMBLES WITH OKARA

MAKES ABOUT 1½ POUNDS
(750G)

¾ cup (108g) quick-cooking steel-cut oats

6 to 8 large dried shiitake mushrooms (depending on size)

½ ounce (15g) dried porcini mushrooms

2 cups (200g) walnuts

½ onion, roughly chopped

3 garlic cloves, peeled but whole

6 ounces (170g) cremini or button mushrooms, quartered

2 tablespoons olive oil

1 cup (about 200g) okara leftover from Rich and Refreshing Soy Milk (page 58)

4 tablespoons tomato paste

3 tablespoons soy sauce

2 tablespoons (60g) white miso

½ cup (60g) chickpea flour

1 teaspoon dried thyme

1 teaspoon dried rosemary

1 teaspoon dried marjoram

1 teaspoon ground allspice

½ teaspoon ground coriander

1 teaspoon fennel seeds

Here's a true "whole foods" sausage filled with fiber *and* flavor. The steel-cut oats and dried mushrooms add some "chew" to the mixture, while the okara (the leftover pulp from making soy or other bean milk) acts as the binder, holding it all together.

SOAK THE OATS overnight in water to cover.

About an hour before you are ready to start making the sausage, put the dried shiitakes and porcini in a small bowl and cover with warm water to soak. You can soak them overnight or for several hours. Drain. You should have a generous cup (or slightly more) of reconstituted mushrooms. Drain the oats as well.

In a food processor, pulse the walnuts until they are very finely minced like gritty sand but not a paste. Remove and set aside.

Without cleaning the food processor, add the onion and garlic and pulse to chop briefly. Add the reconstituted mushrooms and process until they are minced. Finally, add the fresh mushrooms and pulse again until minced.

Heat a large skillet over medium heat. Add the olive oil and the mushroom mixture and cook, stirring frequently to prevent sticking, until browned, about 5 minutes. Add the drained oats, ground walnuts, okara, tomato paste, soy sauce, and miso and stir well. Add the chickpea flour and herbs and spices and mix very well, making sure everything is incorporated.

When ready to cook the sausages, preheat the oven to 350°F.

For sausage links: Oil some sheets of aluminum foil. Form the sausages by rolling them into logs, then wrap each one tightly in the prepared foil and bake until firm to the touch, about 35 minutes. They will firm up more as they cool.

For sausage crumbles: Spread the mixture on an oiled sheet pan. Use a fork to break the mixture into chunks. Bake until browned and chewy, about 30 minutes.

For sausage patties: Form by hand into patties—the size is up to you. Set them on an oiled sheet pan and bake until firm, 20 to 30 minutes.

NO-WASTE CRACKERS

MAKES 1¼ TO 1½ HALF-SHEET PANS OF CRACKERS (ABOUT 1 POUND/450G)

1 cup (about 185g) leftover pulp from making milk or cheese (almond, pumpkin seed, hemp, watermelon seed kernels, or any mixture; pages 44 to 54)

½ cup (110g) extra-virgin olive oil

1 cup (120g) flour of your choice (all-purpose, gluten-free, oat, amaranth)

1 teaspoon fine sea salt

1 teaspoon baking powder

About ½ teaspoon flaky sea salt, for sprinkling

2 tablespoons seasonings or toppings (optional): fresh or dried herbs (such as thyme or rosemary), chopped garlic, minced shallots, sesame seeds, and more

These delicious and versatile crackers are as popular as the cheese I serve them with. They have definitely become my favorite. My family enjoys them as a snack even without a topping or schmear. Because they are made out of the fiber-rich pulp of any milk you make plus any flour of your choosing, you can make them gluten-free or not, and can be as packed full of nutrients as you want by using a flour such as amaranth or oat flour. In fact, I've never found a flour that didn't work with this recipe, although each will yield a slightly different flavor or texture.

Make them plain or season them any way you like with minced garlic, dried herbs, sesame seeds, or even za'atar. You can also make them thicker or thinner, depending whether you want a more robust cracker or one with a delicate crunch.

PREHEAT THE OVEN to 350°F.

In a medium bowl, stir together the pulp and olive oil. In a separate bowl, combine the flour, sea salt, and baking powder. Stir the flour mixture into the pulp/oil mixture until the dough comes together. If you'd like to customize with your favorite seasonings, you can mix them in now (or you can wait and sprinkle them on top after rolling out the dough). Form the dough into a ball.

NOTE

Depending on the thickness of the crackers, the color will range from golden brown to deep brown. You can roll them paper-thin to produce very delicate crackers, which will be golden brown, or thicker for a more robust cracker, which will be dark brown.

CONTINUED

NO-WASTE CRACKERS

CONTINUED

Put about three-quarters or the entire ball of the dough (depending on how thick you want your crackers) onto a sheet of parchment paper and smash it down to about 1 inch, then place another sheet of parchment on top. Roll the dough to the size of the half-sheet pan. Remove the top sheet of parchment and carefully slide the sheet with the dough onto the pan. Repeat with the remaining dough (if the dough was divided) on another pan.

Using a knife, pizza roller, or bench scraper, cut the dough into squares or rectangles prior to baking. Sprinkle the top with flaky salt and any other toppings as desired.

Bake until browned (see Note), 25 to 30 minutes, depending on how thick you have rolled out your dough.

Allow to cool completely. Store in an airtight container for about a month at room temperature or 2 months in the refrigerator.

POTATOES AU GRATIN

MAKES 6 TO 8 SERVINGS AS AN ENTRÉE, OR 12 TO 16 SERVINGS AS A SIDE DISH

4 cups (950ml) Cashew Cream (page 49) or Watermelon Seed Kernel Milk (page 54)

1½ teaspoons fine sea salt

¼ teaspoon freshly ground black pepper

¼ teaspoon freshly grated nutmeg (optional)

3½ pounds (1.6kg) Yukon Gold or other waxy potatoes, peeled and thinly sliced

10 ounces (283g) Fresh Watermelon Seed Kernel Mozzarella (page 115), Kohana's Favorite Cheese for Grilled Cheese Sandwiches (page 123), Potato Cashew Muenster (page 109), or Angel's Sharp Potato Cheddar (page 134), thinly sliced or grated

½ cup (15g) minced fresh chives (optional), for serving

We all need comfort food, and this is a favorite. Thinly sliced potatoes are layered with a rich white sauce, topped with cheese, and baked until slightly crisp. The result is a dish that's a fabulous brunch offering that can also be served as an entrée, accompanied by a big green salad. I guarantee that no one will be able to tell this isn't loaded with cream and dairy-based cheese!

PREHEAT THE OVEN to 425°F. Lightly brush or spray a 13 by 9-inch (33 by 23cm) baking pan with oil.

In a medium bowl, stir together the cream, salt, pepper, and nutmeg (if using) and set aside.

Neatly layer half of the potatoes in the baking pan, overlapping them slightly. Arrange about one-third of the cheese on top. Repeat with the remaining potatoes, then distribute the remaining cheese on top of the potatoes. Pour the milk mixture evenly over the top. Cover the pan with foil.

Bake for 40 minutes. Uncover and bake until the potatoes are tender, the sauce is thick and bubbling, and the cheese is melted and browned, 15 to 20 minutes longer.

Sprinkle with the chives (if using) and serve.

TAGLIATELLE WITH BALSAMIC GRILLED SUMMER VEGETABLES AND MOZZARELLA

MAKES 4 TO 6 SERVINGS

3 cups (750g) cherry tomatoes

5 tablespoons extra-virgin olive oil

1 garlic clove, smashed and peeled

2 sprigs rosemary

1 teaspoon sea salt, plus more to taste

2 tablespoons balsamic vinegar

2 medium zucchini, sliced lengthwise ⅓ to ½ inch thick

1 small eggplant, sliced lengthwise ⅓ to ½ inch thick

12 ounces (340g) tagliatelle

8 ounces (225g) Fresh Watermelon Seed Kernel Mozzarella (page 115), cut into ⅓-inch slices or torn into large chunks

½ cup (12g) or more fresh basil leaves, torn or sliced

Freshly ground black pepper

This is the pasta to serve at the height of summer when cherry tomatoes are bursting with flavor. Combined with summer vegetables grilled with the bright acidity of balsamic vinegar and tossed with melty mozzarella, this will become your go-to dish for summer garden parties. Fire up the grill, put some beautiful grill marks on the veggies, and you'll be rewarded with smiles.

PREHEAT THE OVEN to 450°F.

In a medium bowl, toss together the tomatoes and 1 tablespoon of the olive oil. Arrange them on a sheet pan, add the garlic and rosemary sprigs, and sprinkle with ½ teaspoon of the salt.

Roast until the tomatoes are somewhat shriveled and blackened, about 20 minutes. Remove from the oven and set aside. Discard the rosemary.

Meanwhile, preheat a grill to high heat. In another medium bowl, combine the remaining 4 tablespoons olive oil, the balsamic vinegar, and remaining ½ teaspoon salt and whisk well. Toss the zucchini and eggplant in the mixture to coat. Reduce the grill to medium heat and add the vegetables to the grill (you should have about 3 tablespoons of the oil/vinegar mixture left; set this aside). Grill the vegetables until tender and nice grill marks are formed on both sides. Allow to cool briefly, then cut the veggies into ½-inch pieces. Taste, and if you feel the veggies need more salt, sprinkle with salt to taste. Put the grilled vegetables and roasted tomatoes in a large, deep pan and set aside.

While the vegetables are being grilled, bring a large pot of salted water to a boil. Add the tagliatelle to the boiling water and cook until very al dente; do not overcook. Do not drain: As soon as the pasta is al dente, use tongs to quickly transfer the pasta to the pan with the vegetables and toss. Turn on the heat to high at this point. Now add the mozzarella, the reserved oil/vinegar mixture, and ½ to 1 cup (120ml to 240ml) pasta cooking water to create a sauce that enrobes the pasta. The heat of the pasta will slightly melt the mozzarella. Stir in the basil and a pinch of pepper. Serve immediately.

> ### NOTE
>
> *Feel free to substitute fettuccine, spaghetti, or another pasta for the tagliatelle.*

CACIO E PEPE

MAKES 2 OR 3 SERVINGS

Fine sea salt

8 ounces (225g) spaghetti

¼ cup (60ml) olive oil

1½ to 2 tablespoons coarsely crushed black pepper, to taste

6 ounces (170g) Overnight in Parma (page 128) or Parmacasio (page 147), grated, plus more for serving

Cacio e pepe (cheese and pepper) is basically a sophisticated adult's version of mac and cheese. This traditional Roman plate of spaghetti seasoned with just two things—cheese and pepper—is both comforting and exciting. To make this right, you need ample crushed or coarsely ground black pepper (yes, it's peppery!). I like to use a mortar and pestle (or a heavy wine bottle!) to crush it before using, but you can use store-bought coarsely ground pepper as well.

BRING A LARGE big pot of salted water to a boil. Add the spaghetti and cook 2 to 3 minutes shy of al dente. (Generally, package directions will have the pasta cooked al dente or even softer. For this recipe, you want a "bite" in the middle because it will continue to cook in the skillet.)

About 3 minutes before the pasta is ready, heat a skillet over medium-high heat. Add the olive oil and heat for a minute. Add the black pepper and let it sizzle for a minute. By this time, the pasta should be ready to go.

Use a pair of tongs to transfer the spaghetti to the skillet directly from the pot. Reserve the pasta water. Add the cheese and stir. Add some pasta water—start with ½ cup (120ml) and stir and toss to make a cheesy sauce, adding more pasta water until you have a beautiful sauce that enrobes the pasta.

Serve immediately with more grated Parm and salt to taste.

NOTE

Make sure all your ingredients are ready to go before you start, because this dish comes together very fast.

NO-WASTE CHOCOLATE CHIP COOKIES

MAKES 36 COOKIES

1 cup (225g) Baking and Culinary Butter (page 70) or store-bought nondairy butter, at room temperature

¾ cup (145g) coconut sugar

¾ cup (145g) brown sugar

3 tablespoons any vegan yogurt (homemade, pages 79 to 93, or store-bought) or sour cream (homemade, page 74, or store-bought)

1 cup (about 185g) leftover pulp from making milk (almond, pumpkin seed, hemp, watermelon seed kernels, or any mixture; pages 44 to 54)

1 cup (120g) all-purpose or gluten-free flour

2 tablespoons finely ground coffee

1 teaspoon baking powder

½ teaspoon baking soda

½ teaspoon fine sea salt

1 teaspoon vanilla extract

10 ounces (285g) vegan chocolate chips

No, these cookies aren't just a way to use up leftover pulp but could be the excuse to make some milk—yes, you can have your milk and cookies, too! The pulp makes them tender and moist inside while the edges have a delicate crunch.

PREHEAT THE OVEN to 350°F. Line two sheet pans with parchment paper.

In a stand mixer fitted with the paddle, beat the butter, coconut sugar, and brown sugar until creamy. Add the yogurt or sour cream and beat well, then beat in the pulp. In a separate bowl, sift together the flour, coffee, baking powder, baking soda, and salt. Add to the butter/pulp mixture and mix well. Add the vanilla and chocolate chips and mix again.

Using a cookie scoop or tablespoon, drop balls of dough onto the lined pans, leaving an inch or so between them.

Bake until browned, 15 to 17 minutes, noting that a little extra color for these will not mean they are overbaked—they need the extra time to hold together.

Let cool completely before removing from the pan. Store in an airtight container at room temperature or in the refrigerator for up to 3 weeks.

CHOCOLATE-CHESTNUT CANNOLI

MAKES 14 CANNOLI

FILLING

6 ounces (170g) peeled cooked chestnuts, jarred, frozen, or vacuum-packed

½ cup (120ml) maple syrup

⅔ cup (160g) Sunny Cream Cheese (page 99) or Sunny Mascarpone (page 100)

⅔ cup (140g) Almond–Pumpkin Seed Ricotta (page 101) or Watermelon Seed–Cashew Ricotta (page 102)

6 ounces (340g) dark chocolate (70% to 80% cacao), melted

2 tablespoons unsweetened cocoa powder

2 tablespoons rum

1 teaspoon vanilla extract

2 tablespoons cacao nibs

SHELLS

Avocado oil or other neutral oil, for frying (4 to 8 cups, depending on the size of the pot), plus more for brushing

14 vegan wonton or potsticker wrappers

3 ounces (85g) dark chocolate (70% to 80% cacao), melted

¼ cup (30g) powdered sugar (optional), for sprinkling

This dessert is, simply put, divinely delicious. The crisp shell holds a rich, creamy chocolate concoction, and the ends of the filled shells are dipped in chocolate for added decadence. It's hard to eat just one, but this is also the kind of dessert that makes you want to take your time and savor every bite. In this rendition of the Italian classic, I use both a homemade cream cheese and one of the two homemade ricottas.

For the cannoli shells, I use vegan wonton wrappers, which eases preparation. There are two tools I recommend for making these: cannoli tubes and a pastry bag (see Note). Cannoli tubes are forms used to keep the shells in shape during frying (or baking); I recommend that you have three or four tubes on hand.

Make the filling: In a food processor, combine the chestnuts and maple syrup and process until fairly creamy. Add the cream cheese, ricotta, melted chocolate, cocoa powder, rum, and vanilla and process until smooth, light, and creamy. Transfer to a bowl and stir in the cacao nibs.

Make the shells: Pour 2 inches of oil into a wok or wide pot and heat over medium heat to 375°F. If you don't have a deep-fry thermometer, test the oil temperature by adding a small piece of one wrapper to it. If it sinks but rises quickly and steadily to the top, the oil is hot enough. If it sinks to the bottom and lingers there for a moment, the oil isn't yet hot enough. Having the oil at the right temperature is important for achieving a light, crispy texture.

Line a plate with paper towels and set near the stove. Lightly brush or spray the cannoli tubes with oil. Wrap a wonton wrapper around the tube. Brush a bit of water along the overlapping edges and press lightly to seal. Carefully lower the shells (still on the tubes) into the oil and cook until golden brown, just 20 to 30 seconds. Remove with tongs, tipping each shell vertically so any oil inside the tube drains into the pot. Drain briefly on the paper towels. Using a paper towel so you don't burn your fingers, slip the shell off the tube. Repeat with the remaining wrappers.

Fit the pastry bag with a large star or plain tip and fill the bag no more than half full with the chocolate chestnut mixture. Twist the bag above the filling, holding the bag where you have twisted it. Insert the tip of the bag into one end of a cannoli shell and squeeze to extrude the filling, then turn the shell around and pipe filling into the other end to completely fill the shell. Repeat with the remaining shells and filling.

Dip both ends of the filled cannoli into the melted chocolate. Put the dipped cannoli on a plate or wire rack and let sit until the chocolate sets. If desired, use a sifter or fine-mesh sieve to dust the tops of the cannoli with powdered sugar. Serve immediately or transfer to an airtight container, refrigerate, and serve chilled.

 NOTE

Both cannoli tubes and pastry bags are inexpensive and readily available online or at kitchen supply stores. However, you can improvise for both. In place of the cannoli tubes, use ½- to ¾-inch (1⅓ to 2cm) wooden dowels or bamboo cut to 3-inch (7½cm) lengths. As for the pastry bag, a 1-gallon plastic bag with one corner snipped off works perfectly well.

LUSCIOUS GLUTEN-FREE SALTED HAZELNUT BROWNIES

MAKES 16 BROWNIES

4 ounces (115g) Baking and Culinary Butter (page 70) or store-bought nondairy butter

1 cup (185g) packed coconut sugar

⅓ cup (28g) unsweetened cocoa powder

1 cup (about 185g) leftover pulp from making Hazelnut Milk (page 52)

½ cup (220ml) Hazelnut Milk (page 52)

½ cup (60g) gluten-free flour or all-purpose flour (in case you don't care if it's gluten-free)

1 teaspoon baking soda

¾ cup (130g) vegan chocolate chips

½ teaspoon flaky sea salt

Incredibly moist and light but not dense, these brownies are fragrantly flavored with that magical combination of chocolate and hazelnuts. It's an indulgent way to use up the hazelnut pulp from your milk-making!

PREHEAT THE OVEN to 350°F.

In a medium bowl, cream together the butter and coconut sugar. Add the cocoa powder and mix well to combine. Stir in the hazelnut pulp and hazelnut milk and mix well. In a separate medium bowl, sift together the flour and baking soda and add to the bowl with the wet ingredients, stirring to combine. Finally, stir in the chocolate chips.

Grease a 9-inch (23cm) square baking pan and spread the mixture evenly in the pan. Sprinkle the top with the flaky sea salt.

Bake until risen and the top looks dry, about 30 minutes.

Allow to cool before cutting into 16 brownies. Store in an airtight container for up to a week.

RESOURCES

The Cheesemaker thecheesemaker.com

This is your one-stop shop for vegan cheesemaking: an extensive online store with a large section dedicated to vegan cheesemaking, including a wide range of vegan cultures and many ingredients needed for making the cheeses in this book (including watermelon seed kernels). They have some proprietary vegan cultures, including a vegan version of Flora Danica called MinusMilk, a culture that creates buttery notes. You'll find whatever you need for your cheesemaking adventure here, including cultures, molds, annatto, and other ingredients, as well as equipment such as cheese mats, ripening boxes, nut milk bags, cheese wax, and just about everything else you might need.

Shay and Company shayandcompany.com

Organic and non-GMO shea butter, coconut oil, and cocoa butter, available in various quantities from 1 pound to bulk; good prices and quality; woman-owned business.

Pure Indian Foods pureindianfoods.com/collections/nuts-seeds

Carries watermelon seeds.

Modernist Pantry modernistpantry.com

Lots of "science-y" ingredients, including coagulants such as kappa carrageenan, transglutaminase, and others, plus equipment such as pH meters.

ACKNOWLEDGMENTS

Ah, to write a cookbook again! No less one that afforded me the opportunity to stretch my wings "on the bench" to explore and discover more deeply all the things that plant milk can do.

How did it all come about? One day, I got an email from Bob Holzapfel, founder of Book Publishing Company and publisher of *Artisan Vegan Cheese* (2012), who explained that he was stepping down from publishing cookbooks. In a gesture of generosity, he offered to give me the rights to the book. This meant that I could reissue a revised version of it with another publisher or on my own. (So thank you, Bob!)

But in talking to my wonderful agent, Sally Ekus, we realized that we could do much, much more, that I had learned so much since its publication a dozen years earlier, that it really needed a total rewrite. So Sally got busy pitching my new ideas to various publishers. We weren't sure we'd land again at Ten Speed Press, but we had our fingers crossed!

And Sally came through! I was thrilled because Ten Speed is, simply put, just a great publisher, and my experience working with them on my last two books had been a dream. There, I want to thank my editors, Kim Keller and Claire Yee, plus the great creative team led by Betsy Stromberg, who is always fun to work with.

And fortunately, we ended back with one of the most talented food photographers in the world, Eva Kolenko. Watching Eva and food stylist Emily Caneer work to create sets that looked like they came straight out of the works of Caravaggio was magical.

And how could I not mention Joe Yonan, food editor of *The Washington Post,* who graciously wrote the foreword? Joe is one of the nicest, most unassuming guys you could meet, which you wouldn't expect because he's such a badass at one of the most renowned news organizations in the country. He also writes cookbooks, enters sandwich competitions for fun, and leads a plant-based lifestyle to boot!

While some of the recipe development was relatively straightforward (milk, ice cream, baked goods), the work involved in creating new ways to turn plant milk into cheese was incredibly challenging and time consuming. I was also looking for specific cultures that would deliver certain flavor notes and wanted to be able to direct readers to helpful sources. Dan and Lisa Calkins of thecheesemaker.com responded to my email immediately and have helped "set up shop" for vegans. When I told them that I wanted a vegan version of Flora Danica, a culture that creates buttery notes, they immediately put something together and offered it as MinusMilk.

Finally, my ever-increasing band of "taste testers" among my family, friends, and supporters of Rancho Compasión has helped me figure out which cheeses are "hits" that deserved to be in the book and which did not, and without them I could not have made any sense of all my wild and sometimes wacky new ideas and experimentation. And then there were the animals, mostly the piggies (Argon, Gamber, Ginsberg, Goober, Onyx, Oxy, Pearl, Princess, Shannon, and Turk) who gladly ate up and much appreciated the experiments that didn't pass the bar for us humans!

To everyone mentioned here, a great big THANK YOU!

INDEX

TEN SPEED PRESS
An imprint of the Crown Publishing Group
A division of Penguin Random House LLC
1745 Broadway
New York, NY 10019
tenspeed.com
penguinrandomhouse.com

TEN SPEED PRESS and the Ten Speed Press colophon are registered trademarks of Penguin Random House LLC.

Typefaces: Klim Type Foundry's Calibre and American Type Founders' Lydian

Library of Congress Cataloging-in-Publication Data
Names: Schinner, Miyoko Nishimoto, 1957– author.
Title: The vegan creamery : plant-based cheese, milk, ice cream, and more / Miyoko Schinner.
Identifiers: LCCN 2024044405 (print) | LCCN 2024044406 (ebook) | ISBN 9780593836071 (hardcover) | ISBN 9780593836088 (ebook)
Subjects: LCSH: Vegan cooking. | LCGFT: Cookbooks.
Classification: LCC TX837 .S295 2025 (print) | LCC TX837 (ebook) | DDC 641.5/6362—dc23/eng/20241029
LC record available at https://lccn.loc.gov/2024044405
LC ebook record available at https://lccn.loc.gov/2024044406

Hardcover ISBN: 978-0-593-83607-1
Ebook ISBN: 978-0-593-83608-8

Acquisitions editor: Kim Keller | Project editor: Claire Yee | Production editor: Liana Faughnan
Text and cover designer: Isabelle Gioffredi | Art director: Betsy Stromberg | Production designers: Mari Gill and Faith Hague
Production and prepress color: Kim Tyner
Food stylist: Emily Caneer | Food stylist assistant: Carrie Beyer
Prop stylist: Genesis Vallejo
Photo assistant, Digitech, and photo retoucher: Eva Kolenko
Copy editor: Kate Slate | Proofreaders: Eldes Tran, Hope Clarke, Sigi Nacson, Nancy Inglis, and Miriam Taveras
Indexer: Elizabeth Parson
Publicist: Lauren Chung | Marketer: Monica Stanton

Manufactured in China

10 9 8 7 6 5 4 3 2 1

First Edition

The authorized representative in the EU for product safety and compliance is Penguin Random House Ireland, Morrison Chambers, 32 Nassau Street, Dublin D02 YH68, Ireland, https://eu-contact.penguin.ie.

Miyoko Schinner is an award-winning chef, author, entrepreneur, and activist for animals and food systems. Named a Game Changer by *Food & Wine* and featured on the *Forbes* 50 Over 50 list, she is the founder and former CEO of Miyoko's Creamery, a company with products distributed in more than 20,000 stores in North America, and is often credited with having helped create a new category of food. Schinner is also the founder of Rancho Compasión, a nonprofit farmed animal sanctuary located in Northern California that is home to more than 100 animals.